Walks For All Ages Vale of Glamorgan & Bridgend

WALKS FOR ALL AGES

VALE OF GLAMORGAN & BRIDGEND

HUGH TAYLOR & MOIRA McCROSSAN

Published by Bradwell Books
9 Orgreave Close Sheffield S13 9NP
Email: books@bradwellbooks.co.uk

British Library Cataloguing in Publication Data: a catalogue record for this book is available from the British Library.

1st Edition

ISBN: 9781909914834

Print: Gomer Press, Llandysul, Ceredigion SA44 4JL

Design by: Erik Siewko Creative, Derbyshire.
eriksiewko@gmail.com

The information in this book has been produced in good faith and is intended as a general guide. Bradwell Books and its authors have made all reasonable efforts to ensure that the details are correct at the time of publication. Bradwell Books and the author cannot accept any responsibility for any changes that have taken place subsequent to the book being published. It is the responsibility of individuals undertaking any of the walks listed in this publication to exercise due care and consideration for the health and wellbeing of each other in the party. Particular care should be taken if you are inexperienced. The walks in this book are not especially strenuous but individuals taking part should ensure they are fit and able to complete the walk before setting off.

INTRODUCTION

People have lived in this small fertile corner of Wales for millennia, the rocks, cliffs and beaches of the long coast providing food, shelter and recreation. The evidence of the past surfaces in the sand dunes or lies hidden beneath a lake.

It is rich in history and legend, where ancient stories blend into fantastical tales. Evidence abounds too of the more recent past, when in the 18th and 19th centuries this place was a smoking, pulsating hub of the new industrial age.

Although the area is not extensive, the variety and appeal of the walks is astonishing. The coastal walks are bracing and breath-taking, from high cliffs of limestone and sandstone to long sandy beaches and the classic British seaside promenade. The waves are a surfers' paradise and all sorts of boats from kayaks to power boats can be seen in the bays. However, the lighthouses are a stark reminder of the dangers and of how many ships have been swept to destruction on these rocks. Some of them of course were helped along by the false lights of wreckers, who lured the sailors to certain death and plundered their cargoes. You'll hear all about these 18th- and 19th-century wreckers in the surrounding villages.

© Mick Lobb

The 18th- and 19th-century industrialisation of the area, gradually dismantled and abandoned through the 20th century, left a scarred landscape of disused railway tracks, slag heaps, polluted rivers, gaping empty quarries, crumbling factory buildings and precarious chimneys. This has all changed. The rivers have been cleaned and teem with fish, the industrial sites have been transformed into heritage sites or nature parks and the old railway tracks are now walking or cycling paths. The dirt and pollution have disappeared under green swathes of countryside, with bucolic landscapes of meadows and hayfields making it seem that the industrial past is now just one of the many legends.

There are the stories of a town submerged in a lake, reflecting the actual fate of a medieval town buried beneath the sand dunes. Then there was the notorious landlord who murdered his guests, whose bodies were found after his death. Numerous ghosts have been connected to the nefarious deeds of the wreckers. Wherever you go here, you won't be bored and you may even find some of the spots strangely familiar, like the medieval village or the bay which provided locations for Doctor Who.

STARTING FROM A BEAUTIFUL 12TH-CENTURY CHURCH, THIS WALK TAKES YOU BY A RUGGED ROCKY COASTLINE, WITH CRASHING WAVES AND AN INTACT WORLD WAR II PILLBOX.

Llantwit Major has a history stretching back into the mists of time and was once a major seat of learning in the early years when Christianity first arrived in Wales. Missionaries from the Continent spread throughout the Celtic fringes and it was St Illtud who settled here, founding his church and school around AD 500. It would become the centre of Welsh Christianity and the burial place of kings. The church that now stands on the site of this early saint's original cell was built by the Normans in the 12th and 13th centuries.

The West Church was the first part built. It was the original parish church and is entered through a Norman arch, added not long after it was built in the early 12th century. In the 15th century the Galilee chapel was built, originally as a Lady Chapel but used mainly as a Chantry. This lay in ruins until recently when it was rebuilt to house the church's collection of Celtic stones, including the 9th-century Houelt Cross, that were all found in or around the church. The East Church was completed in the 13th century and contains a number of items of great historical interest including the effigies of a monk, an Elizabethan lady and what is thought to be a manor official. The building still functions as the local parish church.

The town has an extensive Blue Plaque Trail. Other than the church you will pass the Town Hall, originally a Norman manorial courthouse where the courts dealing with both tenants and freeholders convened. It was rebuilt in the late 15th century, became the Guildhall during the reign of Henry VIII, and was used by the local lodge of the Oddfellows Society in 1845 until it was taken over by the Parish Council in 1894. There's a 14th-century house that was used as the gatehouse to a grouping of farm buildings that belonged to Tewkesbury Abbey. This grange or estate was also known locally as Abbots Llantwit or West Llantwit. When the abbeys were dissolved in the 16th century it was sold off, eventually becoming the property of the Earl of Plymouth. You can still see the dovecote and the remains of a tithe barn.

The Old Swan Inn has been a tavern since the 16th century. It became a mint of sorts during the English Civil War when the Innkeeper, Edward Maddocks, struck his own coins from brass. Many famous people passed through its doors in the 1930s including William Randolph Hearst and Prime Minister Neville Chamberlain.

THE BASICS

Distance: 3½ miles / 5.7km

Gradient: Some gentle slopes

Severity: Easy

Approx. time to walk: 2 hours

Stiles: Fifteen

Map: OS Explorer 151 (Cardiff and Bridgend)

Path description: Fields and paths

Start point: Car park at the Town Hall in Llantwit Major (GR SS 967686)

Parking: At the Town Hall at Llantwit Major (CF61 1UG)

Dog friendly: Yes, apart from the stiles

Public toilets: At the car park

Nearest food: Several places to eat in Llantwit Major

LLANTWIT MAJOR WALK

1. From the car park turn left and take the left fork along Burial Lane towards the church. Go into the church on the right and have a look at this beautifully renovated church, with its Celtic stones. Leave the church and turn right to some steps. Go up the steps and turn left at the top beside Hillhead Cottages to a stile on the right.

2. Go over the stile and head along the edge of the field to the left. Go over a stile and along a path beside a wall and down some more steps to a farm. Pass the farm to a junction with the road and turn right. Continue on the road until it becomes a track with way-markers.

3. Pass Lower House on the left and continue along this track as it climbs and goes through two gates. Eventually you will reach a gate with a narrow path heading down to the left. Go down this path as it heads to the sea, passing through one gate.

4. You will come to a bench overlooking the beach. If you like you can head down the steps to the left to have a look at the beach, but to continue the walk you turn right here along the coastal path. After another stile you will find a bench overlooking the cliffs with St Donat's Castle on the horizon. Further along you come to a World War II pill box and shortly after that look out on the left for a stile in the wall.

5. Cross the stile and head up a narrow path between a hedge and a wall. Look for some steps up the wall on the right. This is the stile. Cross here and head across the field towards the ruined building ahead. You can either cross the stile and pass to the left of it, then climb the gate, which is tied shut, or you can walk around it to the right.

6. Beyond the building head across the field on a faint path towards the left side of a clump of trees ahead. Cross a stile and continue across the field towards the trees and the corner of the field. Go through a gap into the next field and turn right. Go along the edge of this large field beside the trees and when the trees end continue in the same direction. The field is longer to the right so head towards the corner of the hedge in the middle. Cross the stile here and another one immediately ahead.

7. Follow the faint path across the next large field to a gap in the hedge. Go through here and head for the left corner of the next field and cross the stile. Veer right across

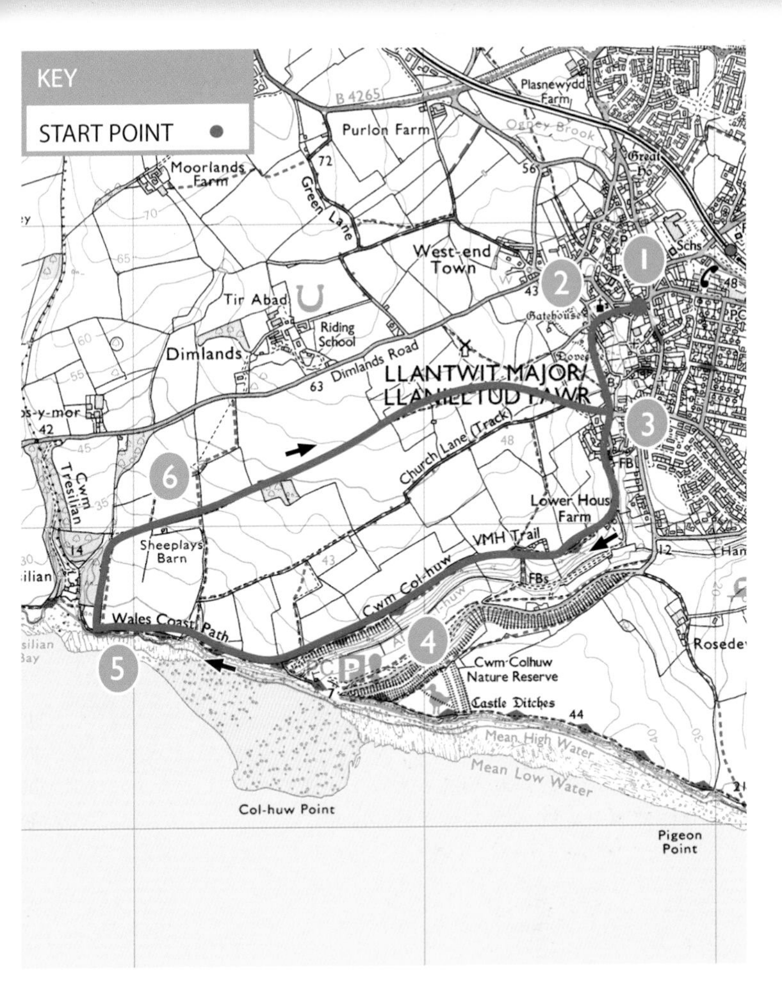

the field to a gate and a stile. Go through and walk down the edge of the field to a stile. Cross this and follow the edge of the next field to another stile. Cross this onto a grassy track with hedges on either side.

8. This emerges onto Church Lane, which leads down to the cottages at Hillhead and the steps back down to the church, from which you can retrace your steps to the start.

MARCROSS

A BRACING COASTAL WALK BY A PAIR OF LIGHTHOUSES, THROUGH WOODLANDS AND HAYFIELDS TO A TINY 14TH-CENTURY CHURCH.

The lighthouse at Nash Point was the last manned lighthouse in Wales. The last keepers left in 1998, they and their forebears having kept mariners safe for over 160 years. The two lighthouses were built in 1832 to warn sailors about the notorious Nash Sands. The Sands had claimed many lives over the years from ships passing the headland. The loss of the passenger ship, the Frolic, in 1831, with 78 souls provided a particular motivation to build the lighthouses.

The higher tower is 120 feet (37m) high and the lower one 80 feet (25m) and until the 1920s they were both lit. By the 1950s the lower tower had been stripped of light and lens and in the 1960s electric lighting replaced the paraffin lights, which had been used for over a hundred years. The fog siren, installed in 1906, is no longer in active use but is sounded for the benefit of visitors, at 2pm on the first Saturday and third Sunday of each month. Look out for the large aerial beside the tall tower, which is a transmitter for the Differential Global Positioning System, enhancing GPS readings for boats which are equipped to use it.

The lighthouse is now open to the public as a visitor centre, one of very few lighthouses to be accessible. It is open only at weekends in the afternoon and a few extra days in school holidays and at bank holidays. Check the website (http://nashpoint.co.uk) for exact details.

Continuing the walk, you pass in front of the sea wall of Atlantic College. This is an International School for sixth-formers, housed in the 12th-century St Donat's Castle. Over the years various owners added to the castle and then from the 18th century it deteriorated. At the beginning of the 20th century it was restored by the then owner Morgan Williams. The most famous owner of modern times was William Randolph Hearst, the newspaper magnate. Hearst spent a fortune on the castle, designing the gardens, importing entire rooms from Europe and installing electricity. He also entertained lavishly some of the most famous names of the early 20th century, including Charlie Chaplin, John F. Kennedy and George Bernard Shaw. Don't miss the tiny church and churchyard of St Donat's tucked away at the bottom of the grounds.

THE BASICS

Distance: 5 miles / 8km
Gradient: Mainly level but some steep climbs
Severity: Moderate
Approx. time to walk: 3 hours
Stiles: Nine
Map: OS Explorer 151 (Cardiff and Bridgend)
Path description: Stony, dirt, grassy and tarmac paths and road
Start point: The Horseshoe Inn at Marcross (GR SS 924693)
Parking: In the village of Marcross (CF61 1ZG)
Dog friendly: Only if they can manage high stone stiles
Public toilets: None on the route
Nearest food: The Horseshoe Inn, Marcross

MARCROSS WALK

1. From the Horseshoe Inn, head down the road to the shore. Pass the church on your right. When you reach the shore turn left through the car park, which is an alternative starting point, and head along the tarmac track to the lighthouses.

2. Go through the grounds of the lighthouses, passing to the right of them. After the lighthouses go onto a grassy track along the coast. You are on the Wales Coastal Path. Cross a stile and continue along a narrow path. The path then goes along the edge of broad hayfields to the left with the sea to the right. Go through a kissing gate and a stile and eventually go into a wood. The path meanders through the wood, crossing another two stiles, and finally emerges at the shore in front of Atlantic College.

3. Go down some steps and then turn left across the sea wall, go down some steps to the slipway and up on the other side. Go to the end of the building and turn left to some steps up to a path going up to the right to re-enter the wood. At a T-junction go right along a stony path. Continue to follow this path in and out of woodland until you come to a kissing gate in a wall. Turn left onto a path, which leads to a gate into playing fields. Go along the edge of the field to a kissing gate to a road. Turn left along the road.

4. Pass the main entrance to Atlantic College and a few hundred yards further on, look for the back entrance on the left. Turn back into this and follow it down to a junction of paths at a car park. Turn down to the right and follow this path down to St Donat's Church. Return from the church and take the first path on the left. This meanders up through the forest. Keep heading up and north on a rough track through the woods until you reach a gate.

5. There is another gate immediately ahead. Go through that to a country lane, passing

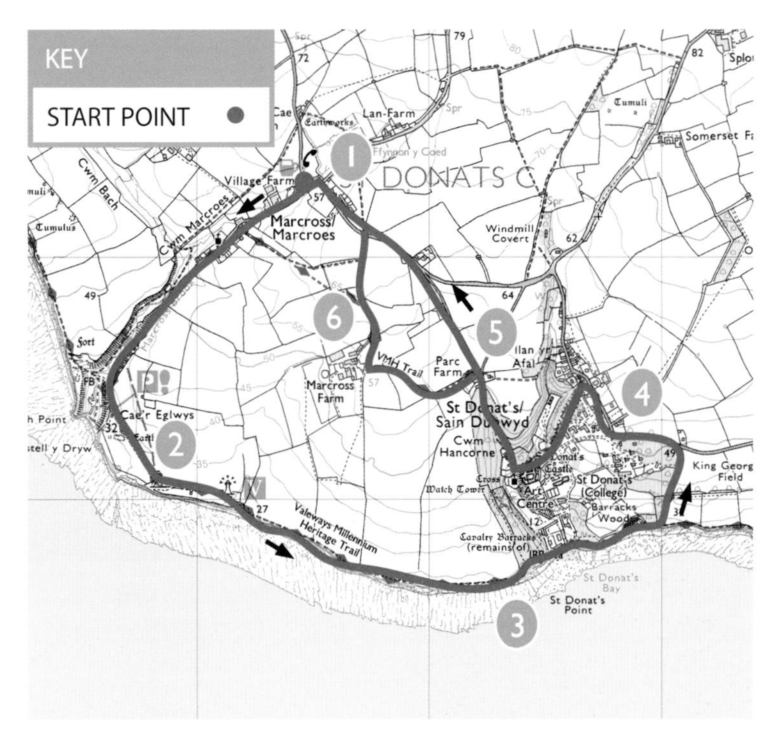

the entrance to Ty Brac on the left. Turn left onto the lane and look for a stile on the left. Cross the stile and go along a farm building, following the path round to the left and then right to arrive at a stile. Cross the stile and go straight ahead along the edge of the field, to find a stile on the right. Cross the stile and follow the clear path straight across the field to another stile.

6. Cross this stile and go straight across to another, which takes you to a farm track. Turn right along the farm track and go through a gate onto a farm road. Follow this to the road and turn left. The road winds down to Marcross and arrives back at the Horseshoe Inn.

A 12TH-CENTURY CHURCH, AN ANCIENT AREA OF COMMON LAND, A FORGOTTEN WELL AND THE GHOST OF A MYSTERIOUS WHITE LADY ALL COMBINE TO MAKE THIS AN UNFORGETTABLE WALK.

Ogmore Castle was reputed to be the site of a hoard of treasure. Many came looking for it but were scared off by the ghost of a White Lady. Then a local man plucked up the courage to stand his ground and talk to the ghost, asking her where the treasure was. She pointed to a flagstone, which he lifted up and underneath found a cavity containing several stone jars each filled with gold coins. The ghost indicated he should take half and leave the rest. But that was not enough for him and he returned later to take the rest. He stuffed his pockets and was heading out when the ghost appeared. He denied taking the gold but the coins fell from his pockets and the ghost attacked him. Although badly scratched, he managed to get away from her and ran home. However, he soon fell ill and confessed to what he had done just before he died. Locals called his death the White Lady's Revenge.

Ogmore Down, which lies between the castle and the start of the walk, is a historical area of common land, where local people had the right to graze their livestock and forage for fuel. Most of the common land in England vanished during the Agrarian Revolution, when the Enclosures Acts enabled local landowners to seize the community land for themselves. What remains here is common woodland and scrub. Locals walk dogs here, ride horses and play golf, as part of the common is a golf course.

After the castle the walk continues along several ancient trackways crossing the common along a valley called Pant Marie Flanders. Marie was one of many Flemish weavers who, fleeing religious persecution, settled in the UK. Her name is also associated with the well that is passed en route. It looks more like a mine entrance than a well with steps heading down into it.

St Brides Church is best left to last so that time can be spent exploring it. This Norman church was rebuilt in the 14th century and was restored towards the end of the 19th. It's dedicated to St Bridget of Kildare and was built on top of a hill on the ancient trackway, The Soldier's Way (Heol-y-Milwr), which crossed Ogmore Down to Ogmore Castle. It had been used by the Romans and then by the Normans.

THE BASICS

Distance: 4¾ miles / 7.5km

Gradient: A couple of long, slow, gentle climbs

Severity: Moderate

Approx. time to walk: 2½ to 3 hours

Stiles: Two

Map: OS Explorer 151 (Cardiff and Bridgend)

Path description: Country lanes, grassy tracks and sandy footpaths. Short road section

Start point: St Brides Church in St Brides Major (GR SS 894750)

Parking: Car park in St Brides Major near the church (CF32 0TJ)

Dog friendly: Yes, apart from the two stiles

Public toilets: None on the route

Nearest food: Pubs in St Brides Major and Ogmore

1. Turn left out of the car park heading for St Brides Church then bear right uphill on a lane called The Shill. Follow it to cross a cattle grid then bear right again at a junction with a farm road. When the lane turns left veer slightly right at a bridleway sign onto the common and a broad, grassy track.

2. Keep ahead on this track, making for the left-hand side of a large patch of vegetation on the horizon. When you get to this observe the warning notices and under no circumstances whatsoever attempt to enter Pant Quarry. Also be aware that a minute-long tone on the warning hooter signifies that blasting is about to take place.

3. Keep following the grassy track between the patches of bracken. Eventually it will skirt to the right of a golf course, then start to descend. Soon it becomes a more visible, metalled track, running beside a hedge and then a wall, then ultimately a tarmacked surface which you follow to the T-junction with the B4524 at the edge of Ogmore village.

4. Cross the road and turn left. Then proceed carefully along the road for a few hundred yards to turn right into the access road and go to visit Ogmore Castle.

5. When you have done that return to the road and continue along it to reach the quaintly named The Pelican in her Piety. At the end of the inn turn left onto a lane leading to the golf club.

6. Then turn right at a footpath sign onto a path that runs behind houses. Very soon this becomes a narrow path that twists and turns through bracken then heads slightly uphill. If it's particularly overgrown you can skip this section by continuing along the road through the village. Otherwise keep going until the path terminates at a junction of roads, lanes and tracks.

7. Take the first left turn onto a track that seems to end at a metal gate. Pass the gate and continue on a fainter track that will curve right along the bottom of Pant Marie Flanders, a steep-sided valley. There are many paths here but keep on the valley floor then choose the easiest option. Pass a stone construction that reveals itself as a set of steps that vanish underground. Please don't enter this. The path

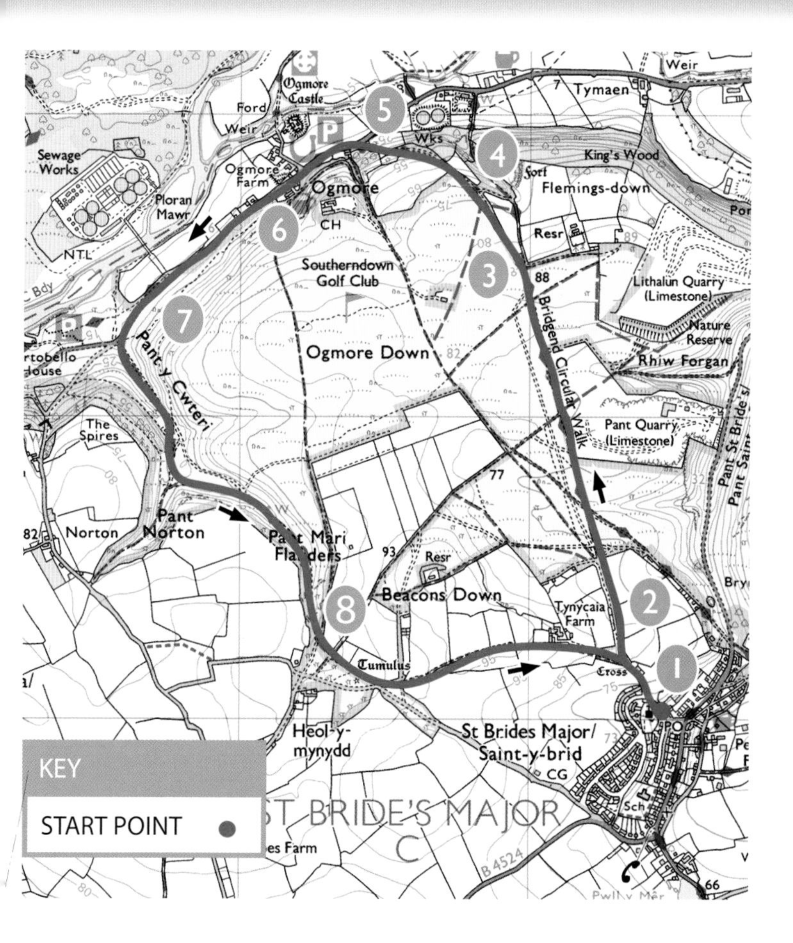

will rise gently from the valley to cross the commons and arrive at a lane by the hamlet of Heol-y-Mynydd.

8. Turn left onto the lane then, when it turns left, keep ahead over the grass by a way-marker post. Then cross another lane and go through a gate. The line of the path is now faint but keep to the hedge on your right, go through a second gate, a gap where a gate used to be at the next field boundary and the one after that. Then in the corner of the final field cross a stile, then continue following the hedge on your left, passing the farmhouse and buildings then continuing along a stone wall to go over a stone stile at the bottom of the field and turn right onto a farm track. At the T-junction at the end of the track turn right and return to the start. Then visit the 12th-century St Brides Church.

SOUTHERNDOWN

Experience an encounter with Doctor Who on this easy walk that takes in a short section of the Glamorgan Heritage Coast before heading inland through the village of Southerndown to Dunraven Park, the Heritage Coast Centre and Dunraven Bay.

You may recognise parts of Dunraven Bay as it has made a few appearances in popular television programs like Doctor Who and Merlin. In Doctor Who it appeared in the episode 'Dinosaurs on a Spaceship', where it was the engine room of their vessel. It then became part of a far-flung planet in 'The Time of Angels' and Bad Wolf Bay in 'Journey's End' and in 'Doomsday', where the Doctor has a tearful farewell with Rose Tyler.

Dunraven was fortified as far back as the Iron Age, when a substantial fort was constructed there. The Normans arrived in the late 11th century and it was passed to the cupbearer William de Botelier for successfully defending Ogmore Castle on behalf of his absent master. His successors anglicized his name to Butler and adopted three golden cups as a coat of arms. In the 16th century the estate passed out of the hands of the Butlers and by the mid-17th century it had been bought by the Wyndham family, who built the Gothic Dunraven Castle in the 19th century.

During both world wars, Dunraven was loaned to the Red Cross and became a convalescent home for wounded soldiers. In the 1950s it was leased to the Workers Travellers Association who ran it as an inexpensive guesthouse, until the running costs became too high. In 1960 it was put up for sale but, finding no buyer and faced with rising maintenance costs for a property they seldom used, the Wyndham family had it demolished in 1962.

The former laundry for Dunraven Castle has housed a tearoom since 1932. Then in 1980 it became the base for the Glamorgan Heritage Coast Centre. The grounds are now a public park, operated by the council and containing a historic walled garden, recently restored.

It's open every day and admission is free. Who knows, you may encounter the ghost of the Blue Lady who apparently appears in the walled garden. This ghost of a young woman was first sighted in the castle during the First World War. Supposedly she left behind a strong smell of mimosa when she appeared.

THE BASICS

Distance: 2½ miles / 4.43km

Gradient: Very gentle. One short steepish section near the end.

Severity: Easy

Approx. time to walk: 1½ hours

Stiles: Three

Map: OS Explorer 151 (Cardiff and Bridgend)

Path description: Grass footpaths, tracks, road and pavement

Start point: The Wales Coast Path south of Southerndown (GR SS 881734)

Parking: Car park on the Wales Coast Path south of the B4524 near Southerndown (CF32 0RP)

Dog friendly: Yes, apart from the three stiles; must be on leads for part of route

Public toilets: At the second car park

Nearest food: Restaurant, tea room pub and shop all passed on the walk

SOUTHERNDOWN WALK

1. Go through a kissing gate at the bottom right-hand corner of the car park then turn right onto the coastal path. This is a broad, faint (but visible well into the distance) grassy track. Keep on it and away from the edge of the cliffs. Then follow it along a section of stone wall on your right and another after that which is part of West Farm and restaurant. When the path almost touches the road, bear left to keep to the shore side of a wall. Although the track is still broad here you are much nearer to the edge so keep a hold of children. Look out for the trees behind the wall that grow at an unusual angle, indicating the severity of the winds here in winter.

2. When this wall ends turn right and follow it to the road. Turn right and take a short section of pavement uphill then continue along a wide, grassy verge to enter the village of Southerndown. Pass The Barn at West Farm or stop for a coffee and something to eat. Then continue, on the road now, and keep on it as it turns left, crosses a cattle grid then turns left again and then right just past a bus shelter. When you reach the Three Golden Cups turn left then, just before the next corner, leave the road and turn left through a gap in the wall at a footpath sign.

3. Cross a stile and follow the waymarks. Dogs must be kept on leads over the next lot of fields. Follow the fence and wall along the right-hand side of the field, crossing two stiles. After the second go down some steps and keep to the right-hand boundary of the field and follow it as it curves to the right and downhill to reach a gate into the woods. Go through this and turn left onto a track. At the end of the woods pass a barrier and turn right to reach the Coastal Heritage Centre, which is worth a short visit. Then continue to reach a car park with toilets and a small shop.

4. Then turn right and head uphill on a faint, narrow footpath that runs beside the lane. This climbs up a short, steepish section with superb views over the beach and rock formations looking back. Then it levels out. Keep ahead to go through a gap in the wall and re-enter the car park.

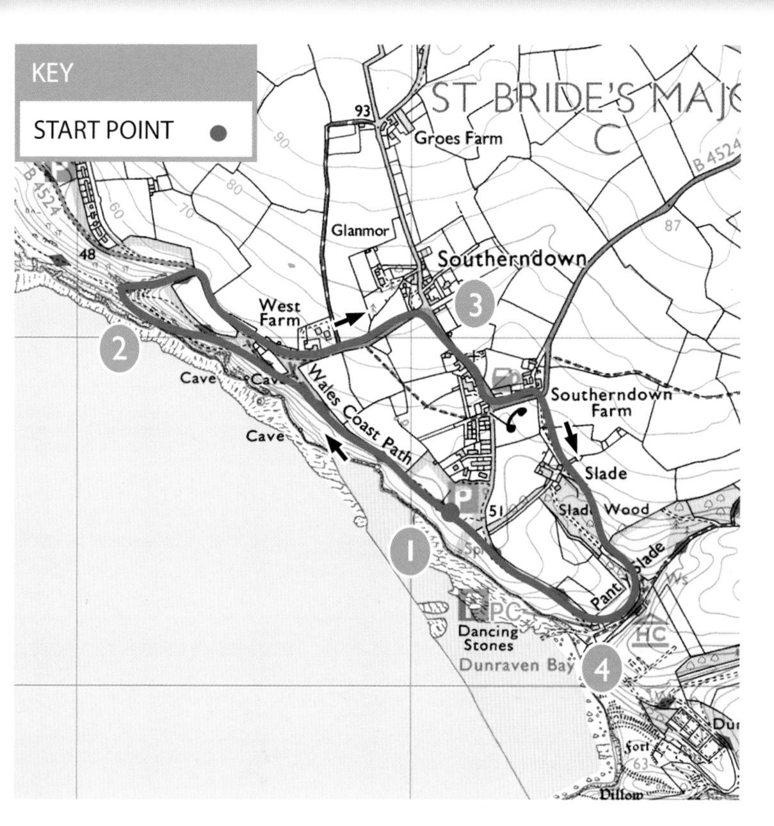
KEY
START POINT
ST BRIDE'S MAJ
Groes Farm
Glanmor
Southerndown
West Farm
Wales Coast Path
Southerndown Farm
Slade
Slade Wood
Pant y Slade
Cave
Cave
Dancing Stones
Dunraven Bay
Fort
1
2
3
4

This takes you through the heart of fertile agricultural land, through rolling hills and fields with glorious views right across the Vale of Glamorgan.

Wick is an area steeped in history. There is evidence of human settlement at Wick since 1600 BC and some of the farming families in the area have been there since the 17th century. It also has some notoriety in its history. The 'Wreckers of Wick' were famed for luring ships onto the rocks with false lights in order to plunder their cargo.

The walk passes through the centre of the extensive Clemenstone Estate, developed by Richard and Bella Franklen in the mid-19th century. It was broken up in 1858 for lack of a male heir. The renovated house, farm buildings and mews here are among the listed county treasures. On the farm road further on, you will see on the right the ruins of the tiny medieval St Andrew's Church. Just along the road on the other side from St Andrew's, look out for Church Farm, a model Victorian farm, also part of the Clemenstone Estate. There are many original Victorian buildings here, including a mill and a threshing barn. Just before the railway at the turn back towards Wick you pass through the gates of the Clemenstone Estate at one of the lodge cottages.

Spend some time looking around the village and surrounding area after your walk. Thirty-four of the buildings in the village are listed as county treasures, including an old slaughterhouse, a cowhouse and stable and a pighouse as well as well-preserved terraced houses. There is the tower of a 19th-century windmill and the remnants of an even older one, built here to take advantage of the wind at the highest point, as you will discover as you wend your way down across the fields with the lovely Vale laid out before you. Take time to have a look at the 12th-century St James's church, which is a Grade II listed building. Don't miss the medieval preaching cross in the churchyard.

If you have more time to explore beyond Wick itself, go to Llampha Court, a listed 19th-century building, from where along a footpath you can see the remains of a medieval village, evidenced by the uneven bumps on the ground. At nearby Broughton is the Malthouse, obviously originally used for brewing, later run by the Quakers to give holidays to children and now converted into flats.

THE BASICS

Distance: 3½miles / 5.6km
Gradient: Gentle slopes
Severity: Easy
Approx. time to walk: 2 hours
Stiles: Twelve
Map: OS Explorer 151 (Cardiff and Bridgend)
Path description: Farm roads and fields
Start point: Wick (GR SS 923724)
Parking: On road at Wick (CF71 7QB)
Dog friendly: On leads only
Public toilets: No public toilets on route
Nearest food: Star Inn at Wick

1. Between the Star Inn and the Village Shop, head along Ewenny Road. At the end of the houses, pass a footpath sign to the right and continue along the road. Pass another gate on the right and then you come to another footpath sign. Turn right here through a gate and go straight ahead down the side of the field and along the bottom edge to a double stile on the left. Cross the stile and go ahead with the hedge on your left, aiming for two posts on the hill.

2. At the posts, continue in the same direction, heading for the middle of the hedge opposite with a barn to the right. Cross another double stile and go straight ahead to another stile. Cross that and head down to the right to the corner of the next field.

3. Cross the stile into a lane and turn left and immediately right onto a farm road. Go along the road here at Clemenstone between two farmhouses, passing a stile to your left, and continue on the farm road for just over a mile, passing Church Farm, Franklyn Farm and Picket Farm. Go through a gate at a lodge and turn sharp right along another farm track.

4. The track bends right at Spring Meadows and then just before the farmhouse at Cwrtnewydd cross a stile and go diagonally across a large field to a double stile at the far corner. Cross the stile and head around the edge of the field to the right to another stile. Cross this and head for a gap in the hedge and then on in the same direction to another stile.

5. Cross this and continue directly ahead across the field to where the hedge turns and then still ahead with the hedge to your left into the corner. In summer you will not see the stile until you are right in the corner, because it is overgrown all around. Continue ahead alongside a hedge and go left at the end to find the next

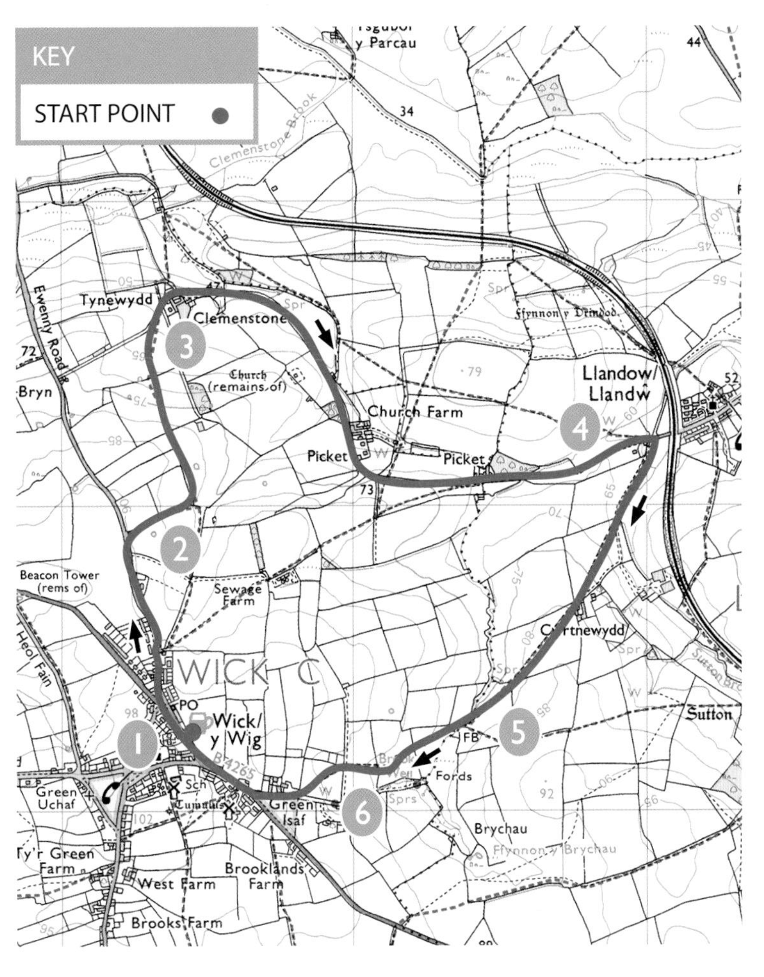

stile immediately on the right.

6. Cross this stile and go diagonally across the field to a stile onto a country lane. Turn right and then right at the road to return to the centre of Wick and the start.

MERTHYR MAWR

GO FROM A RUINED CASTLE FOR A WALK ON THE WILD SIDE TO A VILLAGE OF PICTURE-PERFECT THATCHED COTTAGES.

Before setting out on the walk or when you return have a look at the remains of Candleston Castle. It is the remains of a larger 14th-century fortified manor and the name is believed to originate from the Norman Cantilupe family, who owned it for generations. Now covered in ivy, surrounded by woodland and rich in wildlife, it is an atmospheric ruin.

When you set out on the walk, you will be walking through the Merthyr Mawr sand dunes, at 260 feet (80m) the highest in Wales and the second highest sand dunes in Europe. The dunes extend from here to the shore, on top of an ancient limestone cliff, providing a unique habitat for insects and plants. The area is also scheduled as an ancient monument on account of the wealth of archaeological trove here from Stone Age flints to Bronze Age pottery and burial mounds and Roman tiles. According to a legend, which is probably untrue, the dunes featured as the setting for parts of David Lean's film, Lawrence of Arabia, starring Peter O'Toole.

Merthyr Mawr village has, however, often been the location for films and TV programmes made in Cardiff. This will not surprise you, when you see the perfect thatched cottages clustered around the ancient village green. The 15th-century bridge at the entry to the village is known as the 'Dipping Bridge' because the holes in the side allowed the local farmers to dip their sheep in the river by pushing them through the holes.

The pretty Victorian church of St Teilo may not have the antiquity of the castle or the houses, but it has an amazing collection of ancient stones, some of which were found when the church was being built or when graves were being dug. The earliest of these stones dates to the 5th century, with an inscription in Roman capitals. It is thought from the number of stones found that there must have been an early monastery on the site. Many of the later stones, dating to the 11th and 12th centuries, were found on the site of the medieval church. The remains of the medieval church are to be found beside the church; and look for the early 18th-century sundial, also a remnant of the older church.

THE BASICS

Distance: 3 miles / 4.8km

Gradient: Gentle slopes with one short steep climb

Severity: Moderate. This is not difficult walking but there are no way-markers and often there is no visible path. Ordnance Survey map recommended.

Approx. time to walk: 2 hours

Stiles: Two

Map: OS Explorer 151 (Cardiff and Bridgend)

Path description: Sandy, stony and muddy paths, fields and road

Start point: Merthyr Mawr Nature Reserve (GR SS 871771)

Parking: At Merthyr Mawr Nature Reserve Car Park (Nearest postcode is CF32 0LS) (Merthyr Mawr village); continue on road to Candleston Castle for car park

Dog friendly: Yes, but on lead near livestock

Public toilets: At car park

Nearest food: Bridgend

MERTHYR MAWR WALK

1. From the car park go up the path to the castle and have a look round. Return to the car park and go right on a broad sandy path through the woods. Eventually, as the path rises steeply, it becomes stony and then reaches a T-junction of paths. Go right here towards Candleston Farm.

2. Turn left through the farm, pass a gate on your right and go through the next gate on your right. Turn left immediately and go through another gate ahead. Turn right along the edge of the field. Continue along a wall with a wood on the other side, to another gate. Go through, go to the end of the wood and go through a gate on the right into a field.

3. You now have the wood on your right. Follow the wall to two old ash trees in the field. The right of way goes straight ahead to another old ash tree, on across the next field to the hedge and then doubles back along the hedge to a stile in the corner of the field that you are in at the end of the wall. Cross the stile and bear right to the corner of the next field.

4. There is an awkward muddy gap in the hedge here to go through. There is a stile immediately to the right when you emerge. Cross the stile and head along the edge of the field with the wood to your right. Look for a narrow gap on the right at the end of the fence. Go through to a gate into the wood, marked 'Private', and turn left along a rough grassy track between a hedge and a fence. Follow this rough track until it reaches a farm track and go left towards Whitney Farm. Pass to the right of the farm on a better surfaced farm road and continue down this farm road to join the road.

5. Continue straight ahead on the road until you reach the main road and turn right. Continue round on this road past the church and then turn left at the end towards Merthyr Mawr Nature Reserve. But before you leave take some time to look around the village and the church.

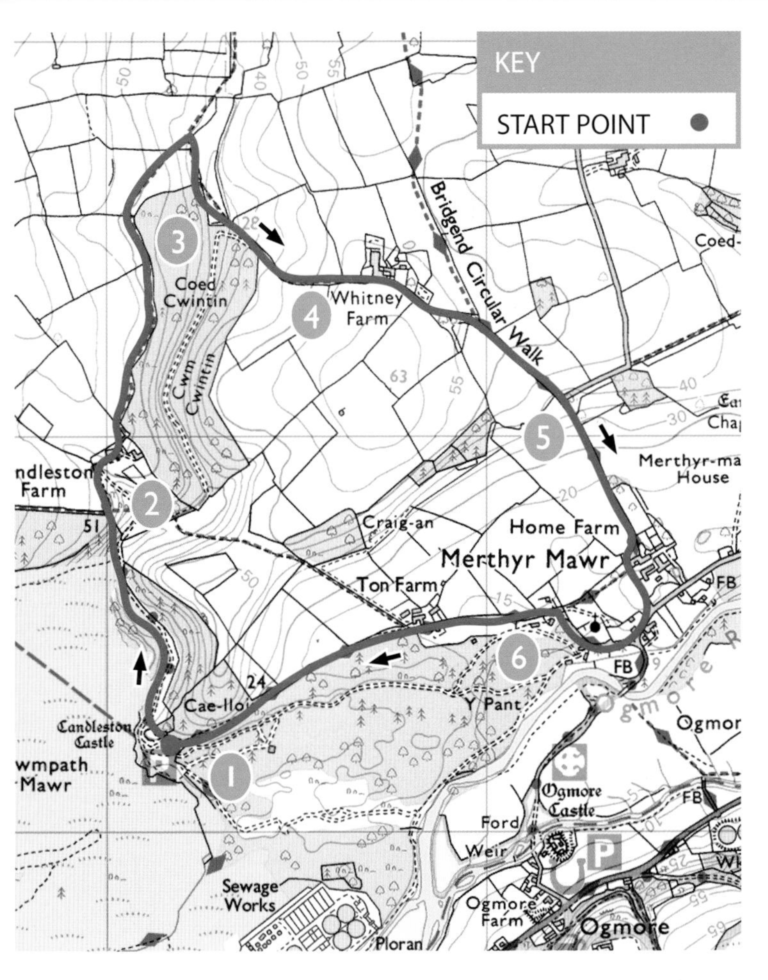

6. Follow this pleasant tree-lined road all the way back to the car park and the start of the walk.

MONKNASH

A LONG-ABANDONED WATERMILL IN THE MIDST OF A NATURE RESERVE, A POPULAR SURFING BEACH, THE REMAINS OF A MEDIEVAL MONK, AN IRON AGE FORTIFICATION, RUINED MONASTERY BUILDINGS AND A HAUNTED PUB MAKE THIS A PARTICULARLY VARIED WALK. AND THEN THERE ARE THE VIEWS.

The Blaen-y-Cwm Nature Reserve is one of the highlights of this walk. A well-surfaced path leads through this peaceful woodland following the course of the Nash Brook. Once a thriving mill was situated here, powered by water from the brook. All that remains now are parts of the walls. The brook eventually tumbles into the sea at Monknash Beach and there are usually a few wetsuit-clad surfers doing battle with the waves.

The effort of the short climb up onto the cliff top from the beach is soon rewarded with spectacular views along the coast. Winter storms in 2013 caused considerable erosion along these cliffs and exposed leg bones believed to have belonged to a medieval monk from the nearby Grange. Because of the precarious nature of the site it was not possible to excavate it but previous digs have established that there was a medieval gravesite in this area. A monastic grange, or farm, was established here about 1130. It belonged to the Cistercian order from Neath Abbey and was active until 1533. Later you will come across its remains, next door to the Plough and Harrow pub. The ruins include what is left of a large enclosure covering around 20 acres of ground. There's also what remains of a massive tithe barn and a circular dovecote with the nesting boxes still visible.

This part of the coast was a notorious spot for shipwrecks, not all of them accidental. The wreckers supposedly hung lanterns onto the necks of sheep to confuse the mariners and lead them onto the rocks. The monks collected the bodies and buried them in the churchyard. What is now the Plough and Harrow pub was where the monks used to store the bodies, awaiting burial.

Unsurprisingly it has the reputation of being haunted by a number of ghosts, including a cloaked man and a young girl called Amy, whose footsteps are often heard. Whatever the truth of the apparitions, the Plough and Harrow is undoubtedly a warm, cosy hostelry with excellent food and drink.

THE BASICS

Distance: 4¾ miles / 7.6km

Gradient: One short, steep section, otherwise nearly flat

Severity: Moderate

Approx. time to walk: 2½ to 3 hours.

Stiles: Seven

Map: OS Explorer 151 (Cardiff and Bridgend)

Path description: Country lanes, rocky footpath, grass paths

Start point: New Mill Farm, south-west of Monknash (GR SS 913700)

Parking: At New Mill Farm (charge), at end of road from Monknash (Nearest postcode is CF71 7QQ Monknash village)

Dog friendly: No, too many stiles

Public toilets: None on the route

Nearest food: Plough and Harrow (near the end of the walk)

1. Turn left out of the car park and head along a lane towards the beach. Then turn right when the lane reaches a track at a gate. Continue downhill then, just after the lane curves to the right, turn left to cross a stile and enter a nature reserve.

2. Walk downhill, along the side of a river, through a delightful wood, passing what looks like the remains of an old watermill, then exit the wood over a stile and continue on a rough footpath to reach the beach. This is a favoured spot for surfers and you will often come across a few dedicated souls here when the tide is right.

3. At the end of a wall, just before the beach, the path turns right, at a coastal footpath way-mark, and heads, rather steeply, uphill on a narrow footpath towards the remains of a barn. It's a short section so take it easy and you will soon reach the top. Now walk along this long flat section of coastal path. The views are outstanding but do keep well away from the edge for it is a long way down. Cross two stiles and keep going until you reach a couple of low mounds with a gap between them. These are the remains of the ramparts of a fort dating back to the Bronze Age. You can explore and see if you can pick out the ditch and the outline of the entire construction.

4. Then turn right, away from the coast, and head towards the left-hand corner of a fence. Go through a kissing gate and continue along the left-hand side of the field. Follow the fence as it turns left then go through another kissing gate, slightly downhill then turn right to cross a stile then continue along a faint footpath to once again reach the edge of a field. Turn left onto this then follow it until you come to a track. Cross this. The footpath now runs across the next field and you can see the outline as it curves gently to the right. Cross a stile into the next field and continue ahead. Again the path is narrow and faint in parts but the line is easily seen. Cross

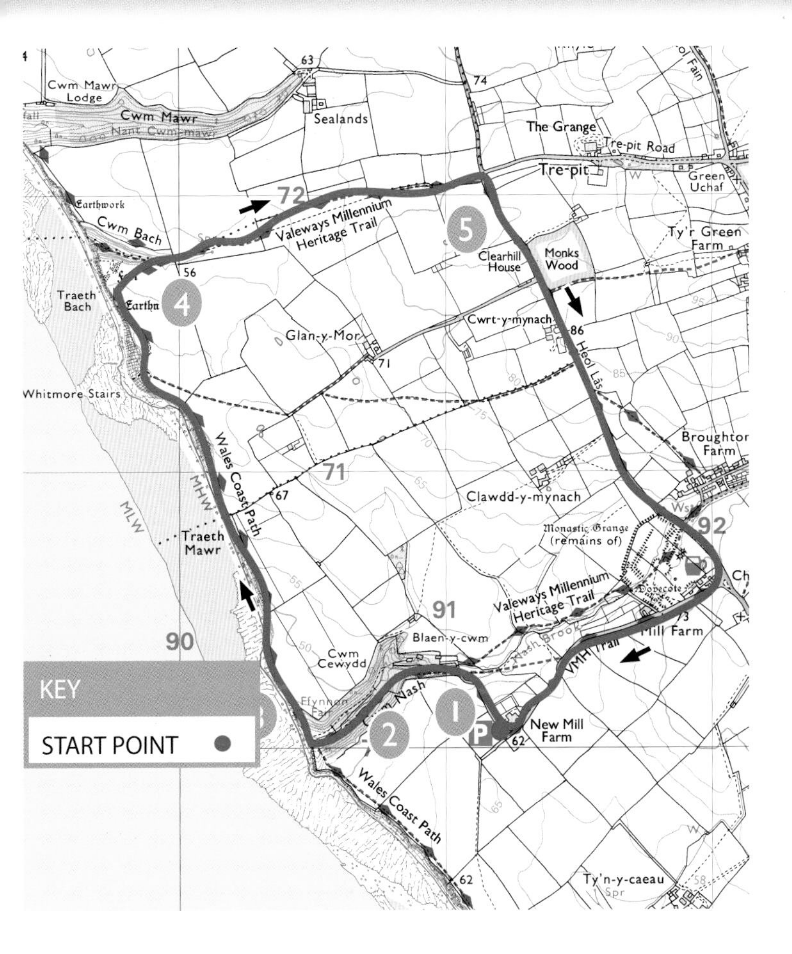

another stile in the corner of this field, walk across the next one then over a stile and onto a shaded footpath with hedgerows on both sides. Cross the stile at the end of this and turn right onto a lane.

5. Follow this for a distance equivalent to that of your outward walk along the cliffs. Pass Monks Wood on the left then keep going to enter the next junction by Church Farm.

6. Now walk along this lane passing the Plough and Harrow pub, or stopping for some food. Then continue past a caravan park on your right to eventually arrive back at the car park.

An inn which had a robbing and murdering landlord, a stone that dances at Christmas and a mid-20th-century stone circle are some of the intriguing stops along this short riverside walk.

The popular River Ogmore is used for many different purposes. You'll see anglers casting their flies in the hope of getting a bite. Groups paddling brightly coloured kayaks and dog owners throwing sticks into the water for their best friend to retrieve. It's difficult to imagine that not long ago this river ran black with the dust from coalmines. The pollution from heavy industry took a terrible toll on the environment, as did untreated waste from the nearby sewage works. Now the water runs crystal clear and supports a wide variety of plant and aquatic life. Salmon and sea trout have returned and the brown trout population has increased.

Not far into the walk you will encounter what looks like a prehistoric stone circle. Look closer and you will discover that it was erected in 1947 to celebrate the quasi-druidic Eisteddfod held in Bridgend in 1948. These stone circles can be found throughout Wales. There are 12 stone pillars in a circle and in the centre the Logan Stone, a large, flat, stone, where the Archdruid of the Gorsedd of Bards stands to make his proclamations.

The 15th-century New Inn Bridge is another 'dipping bridge', like the one at Merthyr Mawr, from which farmers pushed their sheep into the river for their annual bath. Today you are more likely to find people jumping from it into the river or picnicking beside it.

In the 18th century the inn here had an infamous landlord called Cap Goch ('red cap') because of his favoured headwear, who would murder and rob packmen and travellers who lodged at his establishment. He was never caught but still ended his life at the end of a rope for sheep stealing. When the new bridge was opened in 1825, traffic moved away from the inn and it rotted away and was eventually demolished. That was when mass graves were found in the grounds of the inn and the truth about the murderous landlord came to light.

Not on the walk but near the Bridgend Recreation Centre is The Dancing Stone. According to legend, on Christmas morning this massive boulder starts moving and dances to the river for a wash before returning to its site.

THE BASICS

Distance: 2¾ miles / 4.4km

Gradient: Flat with the exception of the climb down to and back from the river on the return leg

Severity: Easy

Approx. time to walk: 1½ to 2 hours

Stiles: None

Map: OS Explorer 151 (Cardiff and Bridgend)

Path description: Footpaths and fields

Start point: Bridgend Recreation Centre (GR SS 903795)

Parking: At Bridgend Recreation Centre (CF31 4AH)

Dog friendly: Yes. This s a very popular dog exercise area for locals.

Public toilets: At the Recreation Centre

Nearest food: At the Recreation Centre

BRIDGEND WALK

1. With the Recreation Centre behind you walk to the far left corner of the car park to go up some steps and cross a footbridge over the river. Then turn right onto a footpath. The path continues beside a lane. When it reaches another footbridge, bear right and continue to enter a public park.

2. When the footpath forks, keep right to follow the line of the river. Pass a stone circle on the left (or make a small detour to see if you can find out what it is all about). Then pass a series of outdoor gym spots where you can try the exercises listed on the accompanying signs. The path comes to the end of the park and continues to follow the river on a well-surfaced track which soon becomes just grass. Keep going along the riverside until you reach a sign pointing left.

3. Turn left to follow the direction of the sign onto the permissive path that takes you through a tunnel under the A48. Then turn right and follow the footpath to reach a kissing gate. Go through this and head along a broad, grassy track, then go through a kissing gate and turn right to cross the New Inn Bridge.

4. At the end of the bridge, at a footpath sign, turn right over a stile and onto a footpath that goes through woodland. When this reaches the A48 cross over, but take great care, particularly if you have children with you.

5. Go past the sign for Pandy Farm then turn left before the farm gates, go through a kissing gate and then turn right onto a footpath that heads towards a metal gate. Go through the gate and bear right along the footpath, which runs behind some houses. Keep on the long straight footpath until you reach a junction. You now have choices. You can keep ahead on this fairly level path or bear right, and go downhill through the woods to reach the riverbank. Then follow it through the Nature Reserve until the path ends at a set of step. You now have several sets of steps to climb up to return to the footpath. When you reach it turn right. Continue along the path, go through a gate and exit the reserve.

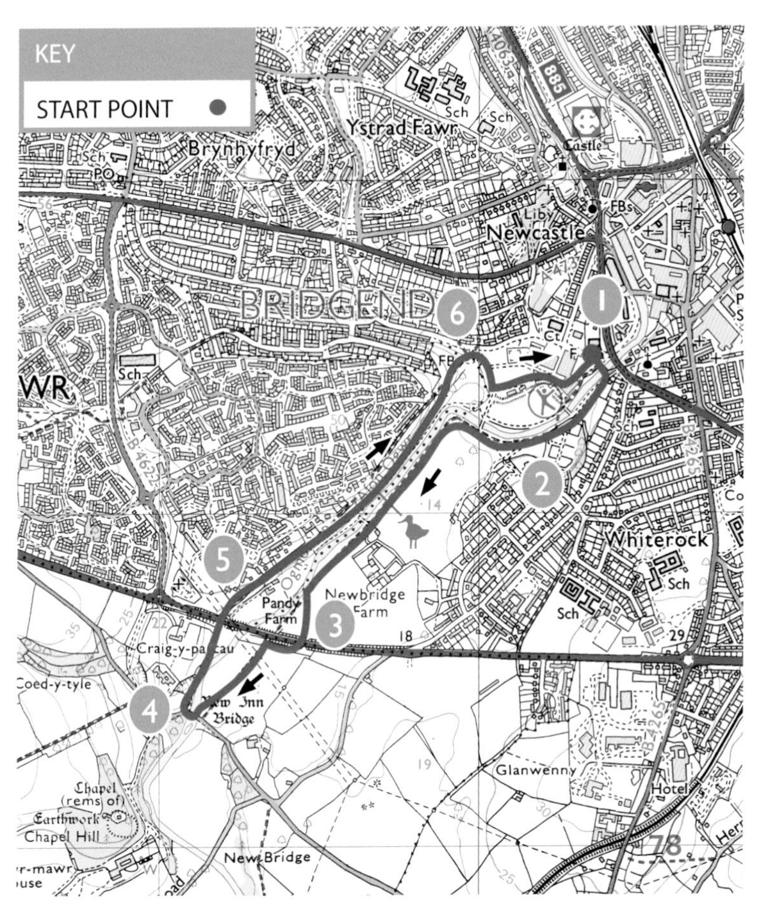

6. The path soon joins a walking/cycle trail. Keep on the right-hand side and follow it downhill, then cross the Pilgrims Way footbridge and turn right, heading back towards the park. At the next junction bear right and follow this path, anti-clockwise, round the railings of a sports ground, past a children's play area on the left and the park on your right. The path now curves right again to skirt the Recreation Centre before arriving back at the car park.

MERTHYR MAWR WARREN

THIS WALK HAS ALL THE ATMOSPHERE OF A REMOTE WILDERNESS WALK BUT WITH NONE OF THE ASSOCIATED DANGER.

The sand dunes of Merthyr Mawr National Nature Reserve contain one of the highest dunes in Europe. Locals call it 'The Big Dipper'. These dunes are unusual in that they were formed against a plateau of limestone, and this is what helped create their unusual height. Underneath the sand most of the dune is in fact rock. Standing on top of the dunes provides incredible views across the entire reserve. And it's from here that you will have the best chance of spotting Burrows Well, a water feature that is not found elsewhere in Britain. Water from a spring works its way through the limestone to emerge in hollows in the sand. Look for a series of marshy hollows. These mark the line of the watercourse. But mostly you will be walking between the dunes, and depending on the time of day you can enjoy an almost eerie sensation of total isolation.

Humans lived here countless millennia ago and the dunes are a scheduled ancient monument. Mesolithic people have left behind stone axes, beakers and flints. Neolithic pottery has been uncovered as well as hearths from the Iron Age, Bronze Age burial chambers and Roman coins. Humans may no longer live here but the place is teeming with life. Invertebrates love the sand and the climate, which is unusually sunny. In summer you can see red-caped cinnabar moths, six-spot burnet moths and lots of butterflies including dingy skippers, small and common blue and small heath. It is also home to rare cuckoo bees, lacewings and longhorn beetles. The abundant plant life adds splashes of colour to the landscape. Violets and seaside pansies, trefoils, orchids, and rosebay willowherb are all present at different times. Later in the year there's autumn gentian and ladies tresses and you'll even come across fungi in autumn in the grassland.

Trees and bushes have got a foothold and are gradually changing the reserve into woodland. To combat that grazing cattle have been introduced to parts of the reserve most infested with scrub in the hope that this will protect the habitat of the rarer species. In winter ponds form among the dunes below Burrows Well and provide a home for mallard, widgeon, teal and shoveller. Waterfowl and waders can also be found along the coast and the salt marsh.

THE BASICS

Distance: 3½ miles / 5.6km

Gradient: Gradients in the warren can be up to 1 in 3. On this walk there are a couple of inclines, which are relatively short and not too steep

Severity: Moderate

Approx. time to walk: 2½ to 3 hours

Stiles: None

Map: OS Explorer 151 (Cardiff and Bridgend)

Path description: Footpaths, narrow and wide, mainly sand that can be loose or compact

Start point: Candleston car park (GR SS 871771)

Parking: Candleston car park (charge); note that this is closed from 7.30pm in summer and 5pm in winter (Nearest postcode is CF32 0LS) Merthyr Mawr village

Dog friendly: Yes

Public toilets: At car park

Nearest food: Bridgend

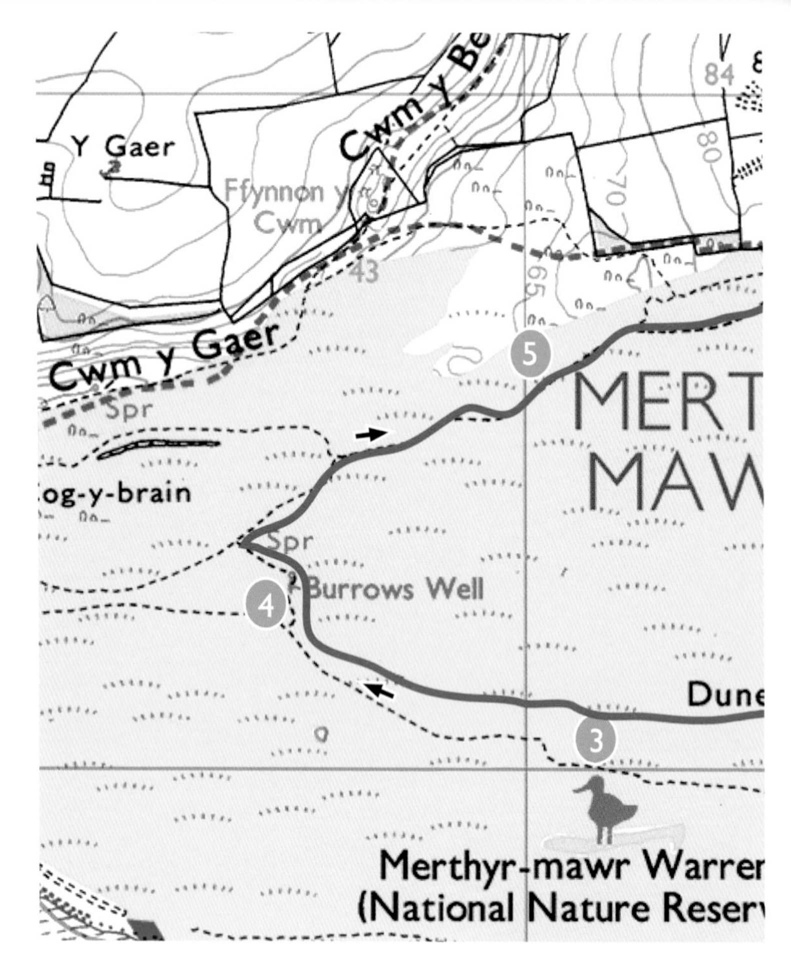

1. Head towards the toilet building then turn left onto a footpath heading into the dunes. Follow the red and green way-marks. Enter a large sandy area and turn right to skirt the edge of the sand then turn right at the next red and green marker. Continue along a footpath of loose sand. It's just like walking along a sandy beach. When you reach a gate go through it into the reserve. Note the sign about cattle grazing and pay particular attention to the instructions if you have a dog.

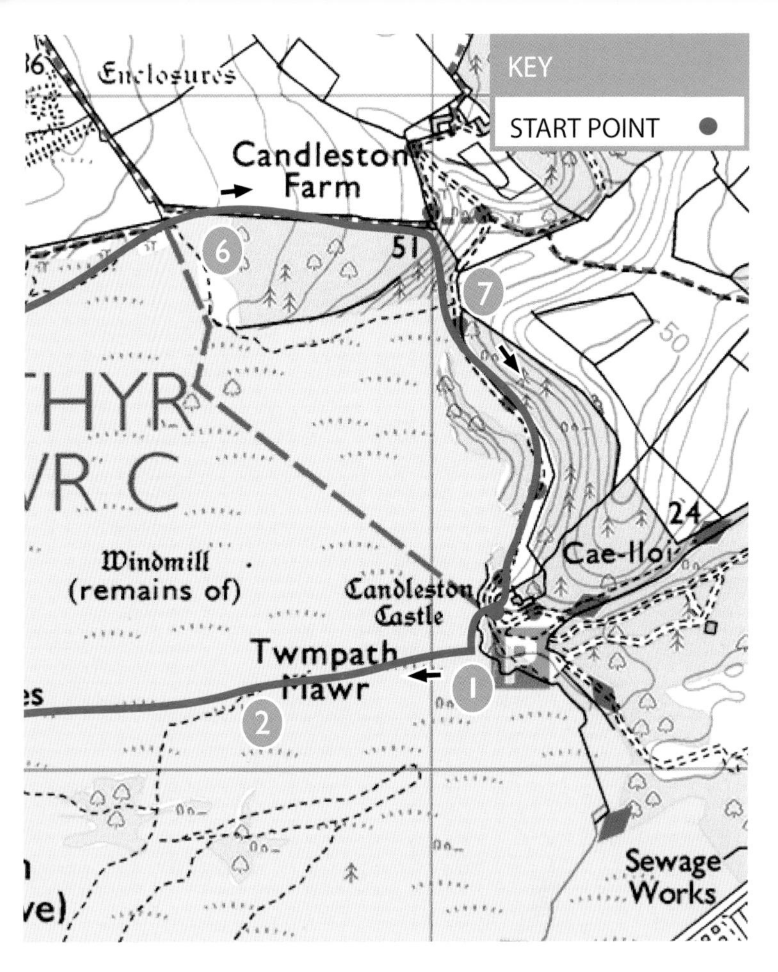

2. Continue to a junction of paths and bear right at the way-marker to head gently uphill. Then pass through some woodland to reach an open area where a way-marker post indicate another right turn.

3. You are now on a much narrower footpath heading gently uphill, then through woodland. Keep left at the next way-marker, continue through woodland, then follow the path along the side of a wire fence when it emerges onto open ground.

Periodically, just when you think you are hopelessly lost, way-markers will appear to reassure you. But keep the fence to your immediate right and you will be fine. Go through another metal gate and continue along the path past a way-marker to reach a T-junction at another marker. You have the option here of going right or left.

4. Turn right and head uphill on what is the steepest incline of the walk. Take it slowly and turn back often to enjoy the views over the reserve, the village of Ogmore to your left and Porthcawl on the right. Eventually you will reach the top, where you go through a kissing gate.

5. Turn right and follow the broad sandy path. Various options will present themselves along this route. They all end up at the same place, but try sticking to the main path. Eventually this will enter a wood, widen to a track and come to a junction just before a gate where a way-marker on the left indicates that you have re-joined the green route.

6. Bear right onto a path through the trees. Keep on this to go through a kissing gate at the edge of the reserve. Turn left then right onto a well-surfaced track.

7. Follow this now to reach Candleston Farm. Just before the farm buildings a track

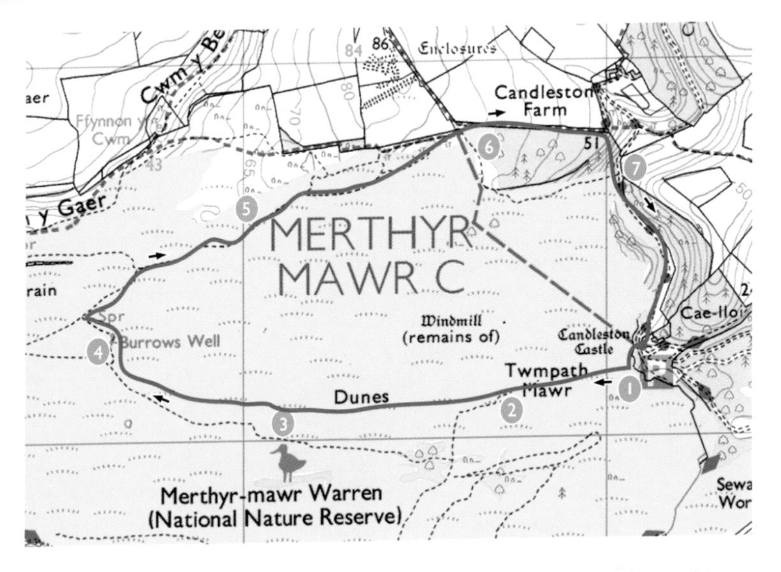

turns right to head downhill on a rocky track. Keep on this as it twists and turns, becomes a soft sandy track again and then arrives back in the car park.

YOU CAN VIEW THE INDUSTRIAL CENTRE OF THE QUARRIES AND CROSS THE M4 BY A NETWORK OF PRETTY GREEN LANES. THIS IS A FASCINATING WALK THROUGH HISTORY, WITH DETAILED INFORMATION ON BOARDS AS TO HOW THE LANDSCAPE HAS CHANGED.

The walk starts along the old railway track, which ran from the port at Porthcawl to the various ironworks. It was originally a narrow-gauge railway on which the trucks were drawn by horses so the 16-mile (26km) uphill journey from the port took 2¼ hours more than the 6¼ hours back. It started to take passengers in 1836 and when the horses gave way to steam in 1861 it became very popular for day trippers to the seaside. The service continued right on until the 1960s, when it fell to Beeching's axe, which decimated the railway lines of the country. There used to be a level crossing here and you can still see the old gatekeeper's house and the building which was once the Horse and Tram public house.

The limestone in this area has been captured and used for centuries, at least since Roman times. Lime kilns produced mortar and lime-wash for builders and quicklime for agriculture. But serious industrial quarrying did not start until 1841, as the demand for lime had increased from the ironworks and easy transport was available by the railway. Although the ironworks had closed by the end of the 19th century, the quarries continue to produce lime on a smaller scale, while the abandoned quarries have become green and pleasant lands, including the 'Blue Lagoon', a former quarry, now flooded. You pass close by one of the remaining working quarries at Pant Mawr and if you stop to have a look at the massive works it is easy to imagine how different this whole landscape would have looked under the pall of smoke and dust created by trains and explosives.

The next part of the walk follows the historic main road from the ancient city of Kenfig to Cardiff, believed to have been originally part of a Roman road. However. Heol-y-Sheet became a byway after the decline of Kenfig in the 15th century. Cut off by modern road development, it is now a cul-de-sac leading only to a farm, although the farm, Ty Tanglwyst figures in 13th-century documents as Tangeuestel's Land.

THE BASICS

Distance: 3 miles / 4.8km

Gradient: Mainly flat, a few gentle slopes

Severity: Easy

Approx. time to walk: 2 hours

Stiles: None

Map: OS Explorer 151 (Cardiff and Bridgend)

Path description: Tarmac, field and some rough paths

Start point: Telephone box on Porthcawl Road in South Cornelly (GR SS 819805)

Parking: On street in South Cornelly (CF33 4RG)

Dog friendly: Yes

Public toilets: None on route

Nearest food: There are plenty of places to eat in Porthcawl

1. Head up the road opposite the telephone box to a right turn onto a footpath at the top of the street. The Three Horseshoes Pub used to be here at the old railway but it has been converted into accommodation. Go up the footpath, looking out on the left for lots of hens, chicks and ducks in a garden to the right. The tarmac path ends and you continue through an A-frame onto a narrow path.

2. Continue on the path past the quarries with a wire fence to the left until you arrive at quarry gates to left and right. Pass these and follow the road ahead to a café in a Portakabin. Go up the steps to the café and pass to the right of it on to a path.

3. Pass a tarmac parking area to the right and continue on the path to a T-junction with a gravel track and turn left. Very shortly you cross a works track to reach a footpath to the left.

4. Go along, then turn right and go through a kissing gate into a field. Cross this field and the next three, following the line of the power cables and going through gates to arrive at a road.

5. This is Heol-y-Sheet, which was the ancient main road to Cardiff. Turn left and continue along through a kissing gate until a footpath forks off to the right. Follow this pretty green path down and turn right through a kissing gate to cross the motorway. Follow it on down to go right under the motorway and then curve up and over the motorway again.

6. The path now heads up between fences to a kissing gate and out onto a street of residential housing. This is still Heol-y-Sheet, which the motorway cuts right through. Go down the street, passing Julian's Way and then, opposite Heol Neuadd, take the tarmac lane to the left.

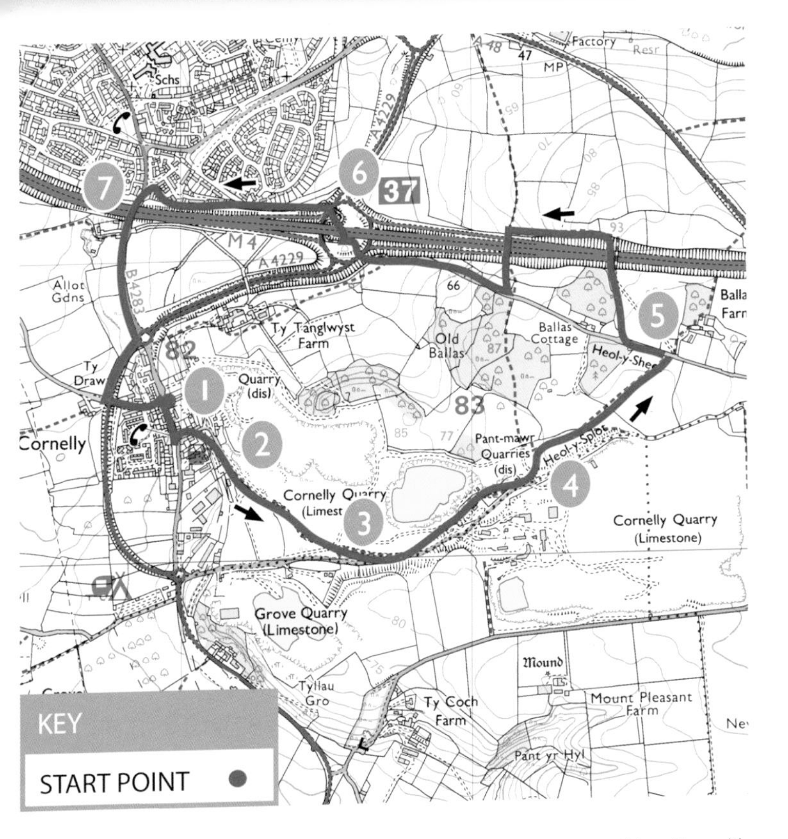

This leads round a play park to Heol-y-Cwrt. Follow this to a T-junction with Porthcawl Road.

7. Cross the road and turn left under the M4. Pass a footpath sign on the right and go on to the next one, just before the roundabout. Fork right up to Ty Draw Lane and turn left over a bridge passing over the main road. At a T-junction turn right to return to the telephone box at the start.

KENFIG POOL

The legend of a Welsh Atlantis, lots of wildlife and a poignant memorial to a recent air disaster.

Kenfig was once a town, founded by the Earl of Gloucester in the mid-12th century. Two centuries later it was one of the largest settlements in Glamorgan but now all that remains is part of its castle. It was a major trade and manufacturing centre situated on one of the main roads in South Wales. It had Guilds of Trades and held markets and fairs. Being a Norman settlement, it was frequently attacked by the indigenous Welsh, who burned it to the ground on several occasions. However, it was finally destroyed in 1439, after several floods by extremely high tides allowed the encroaching sand dunes to bury it.

Kenifig Dunes were formed about four millennia ago and originally occupied a small coastal strip. It is thought that the encroaching dunes blocked the flow of water to the sea, creating Kenfig Pool, the second largest freshwater lake in Wales. According to legend an ancient city lies intact beneath its waters, like the 15th-century town beneath the dunes. Another story to explain the disappearance of the town tells of how the local lord rejects his daughter's impoverished suitor, who later returns with riches, stolen from the lord's tax collector. Although he escapes detection, a curse is placed on the family that vengeance will be taken at the ninth generation. And so it happens that, a couple of hundred years later, when the ninth-generation baby is born, a voice cries that vengeance has come and in the morning, Kenfig is gone and there is only the lake.

But the great fascination of this walk is the wildlife. In the spring and summer, there are orchids, including rare ones like the Fen Orchid; there's Marsh Helleborine, Fragrant Orchid, Southern Marsh Orchid, Bee Orchid and Twayblade. In the winter this water is a haven for migrating birds.

Near here, in February 2009, the Kenfig Air Disaster took place. Two RAF training aircraft, with experienced pilots, taking a couple of air cadets on an air experience flight, collided above the reserve. The two aircraft had earlier taken off from RAF St Athan, 20 miles away, with the cadets aged 13 and 14. The pilots failed to see each other approach and the planes collided in mid-air. The two girls who died were cousins.

THE BASICS

Distance: 2 miles / 3.2km

Gradient: Very gentle, almost flat

Severity: Easy

Approx. time to walk: 1½ hours

Stiles: Five

Map: OS Explorer 151 (Cardiff and Bridgend)

Path description: Sandy footpaths, grassy tracks, boardwalk and muddy sections

Start point: Kenfig Visitor Centre (GR SS 801810)

Parking: Kenfig Visitor Centre (CF33 4PT)

Dog friendly: Only if the alternative end section is chosen

Public toilets: At the Visitor Centre

Nearest food: At the Visitor Centre

1. Leave the car park and walk towards the Visitor Centre. Pass to the right of it and follow the way-markers to go past a wooden sculpture and onto a sandy footpath. At a finger post go right towards the green waymark arrow and Kenfig Pool.

2. Keep on a broad track, sometimes grassy, sometimes sandy to reach the pool near some picnic tables. Then keep left on the track past a green way-mark arrow.

3. You are now on a circular route round the pool. When you come across any junctions, keep to the right and you will not go wrong. Periodically you will get a glimpse of the water as the path passes through various habitats. There are reed beds, woodland, marsh and scrubland. Each one is teeming with wildlife if you have the patience to stop and wait silently. You will enter a section of woodland where the track is very boggy, even after prolonged periods of hot weather. Carefully pick your way through. It does not last long and then a much narrower footpath continues to circle the pool. Children particularly will love the section where the path passes through a section of reeds. They can pretend they are in a real jungle.

4. When you reach a section of boardwalk go onto it and turn right. Follow this to a hide where you will have some great views over the pond, and if you sit quietly for long enough you will probably see some interesting wildlife. When you have seen enough retrace your steps then continue to the end of the boardwalk. Then continue along the path. Soon there will be water on both sides. Look out on your left for the giant bulrushes.

5. When the path divides keep left initially to head uphill on a track, then take the narrow path to the left to climb up to a bench. It's dedicated to those who lost their lives in the Kenfig Air Disaster of 2009. Look out across the pond. This is one of the best views of it you will have as well as of the dune system all around. When you

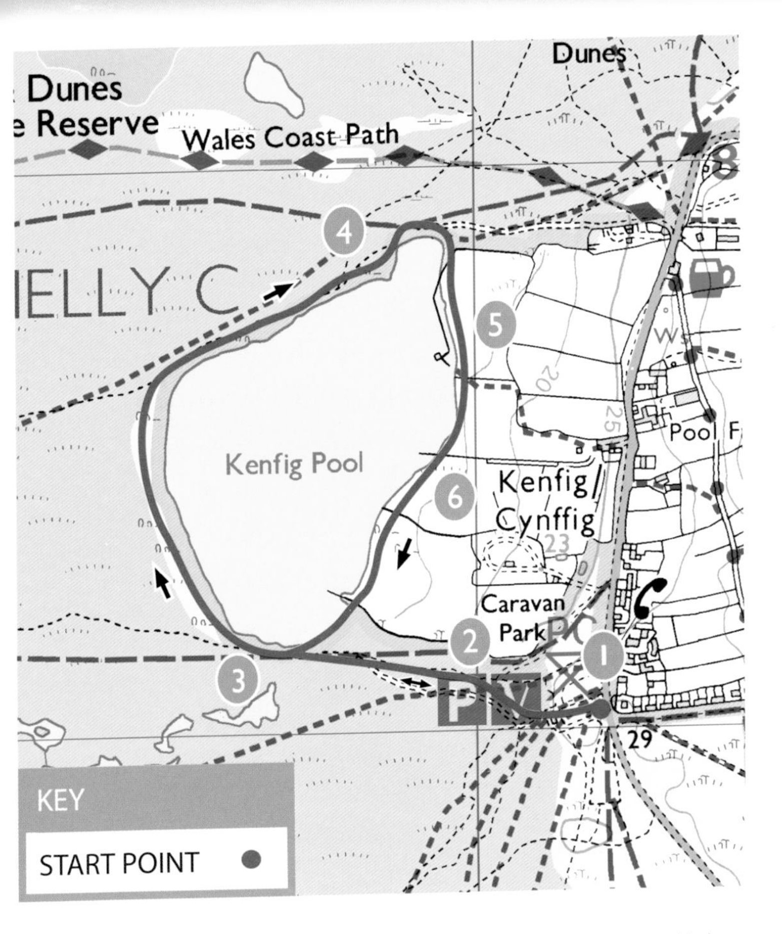

are ready to move on you have two options. If you have a dog you may want to keep ahead to reach the road then turn right along it to return to the car park. Otherwise head back downhill to the junction then turn left along the edge of the water.

6. Cross a stile. This is where you might have trouble with a dog. Bear right and follow the path to the water's edge and continue along it, passing the remains of an old boat house. Cross a stile (this and the next one have dog gates), and continue along the water to cross another. Then keep going to cross a further two stiles with no dog gates. Then climb away from the water on a twisty path through the dune to reach the picnic tables. Turn left and retrace your outward route back to the start.

KENFIG – SKER HOUSE

An abandoned baby and a recently restored historic house are the major features of this walk.

Sker House was a decaying ruin that was finally condemned in 1979. However, because of its historic significance, it was not demolished and finally, in 1999, a four-year restoration project began and the completed building was sold into private ownership.

Sker was compulsorily purchased by Bridgend County Borough Council and then sold on to the Buildings at Risk Trust, who commissioned architects. They proposed a full restoration with the exception of the gable end at its southern end, which had collapsed in 1977. The Heritage Lottery Fund and other bodies granted funding and the work got under way.

Originally the grange, or farm, for the Cistercian Order at Neath Abbey, Sker House dates back around nine centuries. The remains of the original medieval buildings, which would have included a tithe barn, living quarters for the monks and a small chapel, were uncovered by archaeologists during the restoration project.

Following the Dissolution of the Monasteries the property was acquired by the Turberville family and in the mid-16th century they substantially altered it. A second storey was added and a great hall constructed, resulting in the rambling Elizabethan residence that survived well into the 20th century. The Turbervilles lived there until the late 17th century but then sold up. It was then rented to various tenant farmers but received little maintenance.

R.D. Blackmore, the writer, whose most famous work Lorna Doone is still in print, knew Sker House. His mother was from nearby Nottage and he spent time as a child at his aunt's house nearby. He used the house in his novel The Maid of Sker, a title he borrowed from a Welsh poem; but the story is all his. It's a tale of an old fisherman who finds a small child abandoned in a boat. It's a long and rather convoluted story and has long been out of print, although Blackmore thought it was his best work.

Sker House was bought by the Glasgow-born historian, Professor Niall Ferguson in 2003 as a private residence. He has generated a bit of controversy locally by applying to have a right of way footpath close to the house moved for reasons of privacy. Opponents argued that because so much taxpayers' money had been used to restore the property they should have right to get up close to it.

THE BASICS

Distance: 2½ miles / 4km

Gradient: Mostly flat

Severity: Easy

Approx. time to walk: 1½ hours

Stiles: None

Map: OS Explorer 151 (Cardiff and Bridgend)

Path description: Mostly hard tracks, some grass and road

Start point: Near Pyle and Kenfig Golf Club (GR SS 809800)

Parking: Parking area near Pyle and Kenfig Golf Club, on minor road off A4229 just south of junction 37 of the M4 (CF33 4PU)

Landscape: Fields, golf course

Dog friendly: Excellent dog walk

Public toilets: None on the route. Nearest at Kenfig Pool Visitor Centre (see Walk 11).

Nearest food: Kenfig Pool Visitor Centre (see Walk 11)

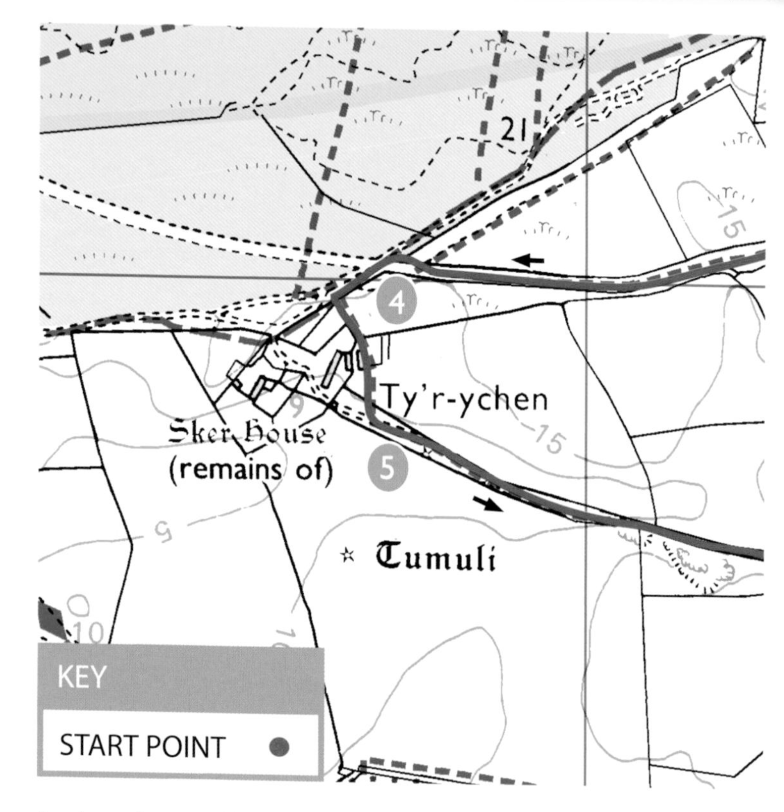

1. Leave the car parking area, cross a minor road then walk past the golf club house. Cross the road and then turn left onto a broad track and head along it. In a few yards turn left to visit the ancient well that has been restored. Then continue along the track.

2. Just before this track curves right to pass a house, bear left onto the grass and head across it towards a kissing gate. Go through this, then turn left to cross a field and exit via a large gate onto a track.

3. Turn right and head off down it. On the way you will pass the remains of an old

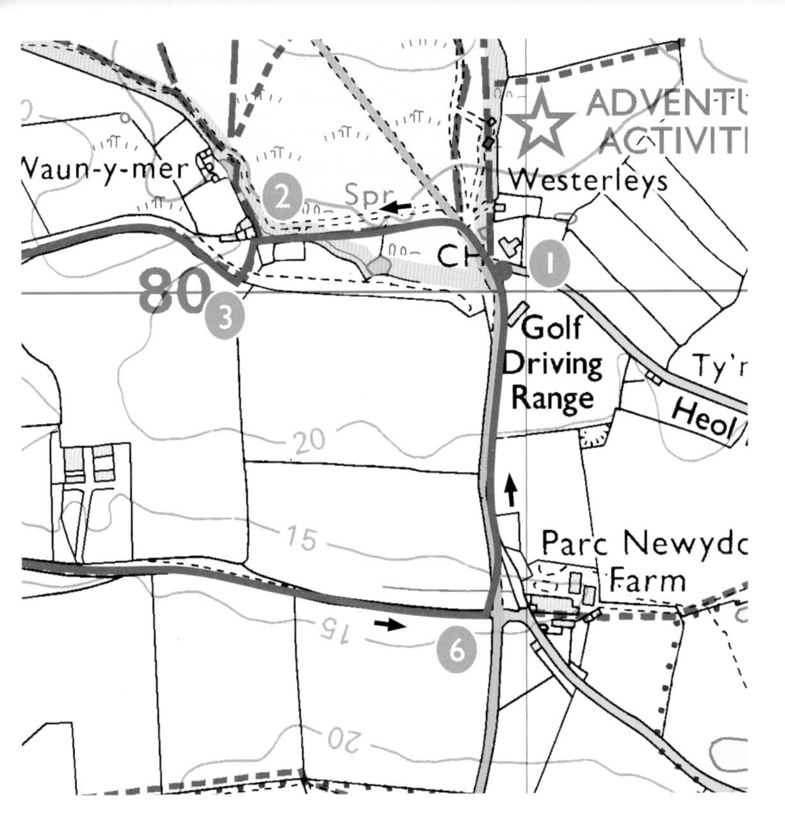

railway goods carriage in the field to your right and then the outline of Sker House will be seen on the horizon. Keep going towards it. As the track begins to curve left towards the house you will notice gates on either side of it. This is where a footpath crosses.

4. Turn left through a kissing gate and follow a broad, green track. But just before it reaches a gate, turn right and look for a small metal gate in the wall. Go through this and head along a footpath, passing a ruined barn on your right. Go through another kissing gate at the end of this section.

You will now have the best view of Sker House to your right.

5. Turn left and pick up a faint track coming out of the broad gate to your left. This curves round to follow the wall on the left. Head along it going through two large metal gates, passing a farm on the left and a grain silo and another dilapidated railway carriage on the right. The surface of the track gets better from this point. Keep on it to go through a final kissing gate onto the main road.

6. Cross over to reach the entrance to Adventures Activity Centre. You may want to check this out later. Then turn left and proceed with caution along a short section of road to return to the start.

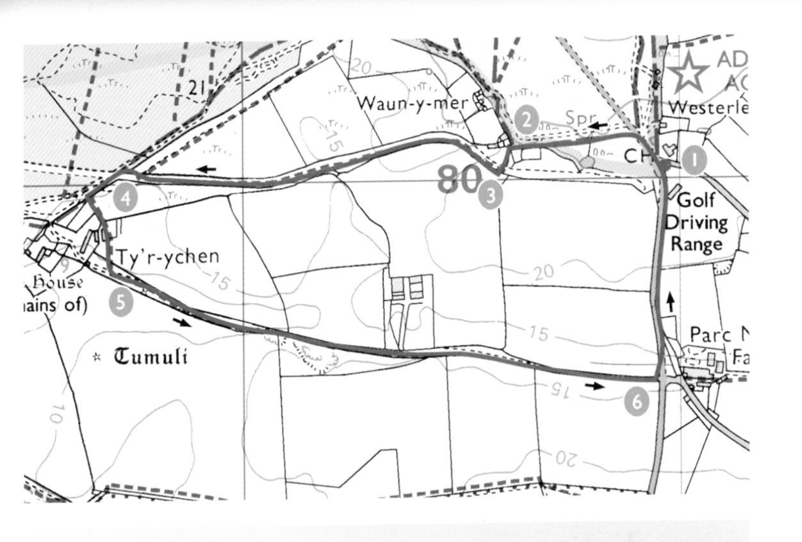
21
20
Waun-y-mer
Spr
80
Golf
Driving
Range
Ty'r-ychen
15
Tumuli
10

PORTHCAWL

TAKE A BEACH WALK AROUND LOVELY BAYS AND AN OLD-FASHIONED SEASIDE ESPLANADE, THEN YOU CAN SHOP ALONG A PRETTY PEDESTRIAN PRECINCT AND TAKE THE ROAD BACK TO SOME GREAT PUBS AND AN OLD CHURCH.

You start this walk on Newton Beach, a long sandy and rocky bay, which is a designated Site of Special Scientific Interest along with adjacent Newton Burrows and Merthyr Mawr sand dunes (see Walk 9, Merthyr Mawr Warren). The beach is alive with walkers, families playing, kites flying and horse riders, not to mention boats and windsurfers. Around the headland you move seamlessly into Trecco Bay, which has very pleasant holiday chalets lining the path. There is a strong lifeguard presence at Sandy Bay at the large orange lifeguard station. This area is classic British seaside. There are donkey rides, trampolines and bouncy castles and, nearby, the Coney Beach Funfair. If the tide is right the surfers will be out in force. Porthcawl is one of the most popular surfing spots in Wales and has a surfing festival that runs in September each year.

As you walk along the seafront, have a look at the Victorian promenade, built to commemorate Queen Victoria's Golden Jubilee in 1887. Restored in 1996, it has cafés, bars and restaurants and a panoramic view of the Bristol Channel. Take a trip on the Promenade Princess Train; eat some fish and chips or an ice cream. After all, you're at the seaside! There is also the Grand Pavilion, another seaside institution, which still hosts varied shows and a seasonal pantomime.

At the end of the pier, you can see the lighthouse built in 1860. It was the last lighthouse in the UK to be powered by coal gas. It moved to natural gas in 1974 and to electricity in 1997. Enjoy your walk along the front and before you turn back have a wander through the shopping centre, some of it pedestrianised, with its collection of quirky and interesting shops.

On the way back you pass the pretty village green of Newton village, with its church and historic pubs clustered around. This is the perfect place for a pub lunch or just some refreshment. The village was originally medieval and St John's church here was built in the 12th century by the Knights of St John. Have a look beside the church for St John's Well, which is supposed to have healing properties.

THE BASICS

Distance: 4½ miles / 7.2km

Gradient: Negligible

Severity: Easy

Map: OS Explorer 151 (Cardiff and Bridgend)

Paths: Esplanade, beach and road

Start point: Newton Beach car park (GR SS 837769)

Parking: Newton Beach car park (CF36 5NE)

Dog friendly: No. Dogs are not allowed on the beach in summer

Toilets: None on the route

Food: None on the route but plenty in Porthcawl

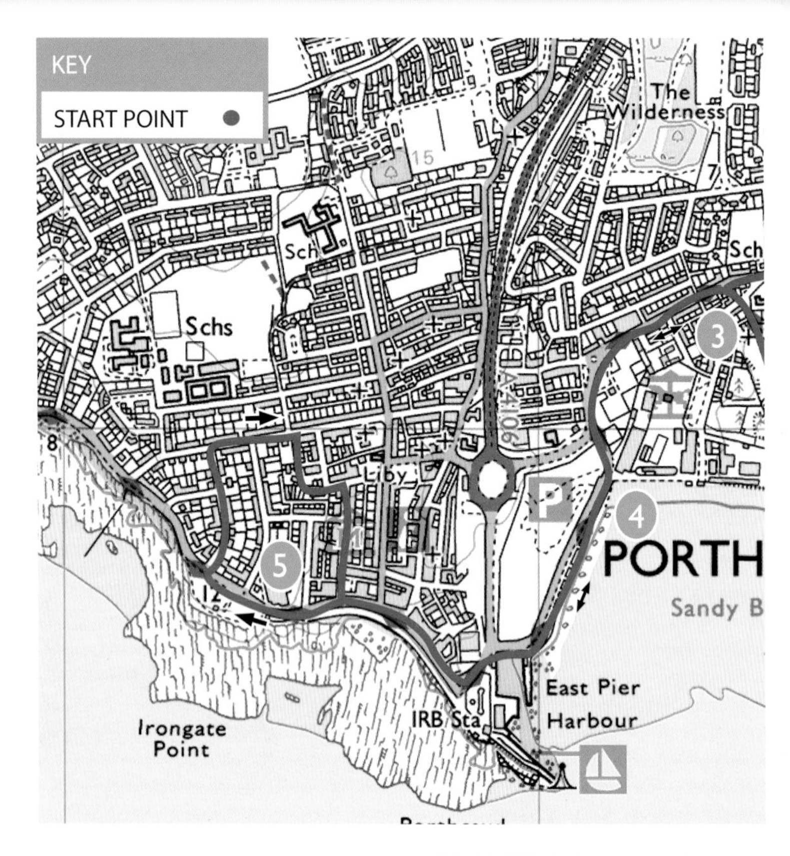

1. From the car park, walk along the road to the road above the beach. You are now on the Wales Coast Path and you continue along this tarmac path right along Trecco Bay with beautiful views out over the beach and the Bristol Channel.

2. At the end of the path head up to the Lifeguard Station, where there is a little path roundabout. Turn left towards the sea and then right along the beach. You are now in Sandy Bay. Walk halfway along and look on the right for some steps. Go up the steps and head straight ahead along a tarmac track, passing a

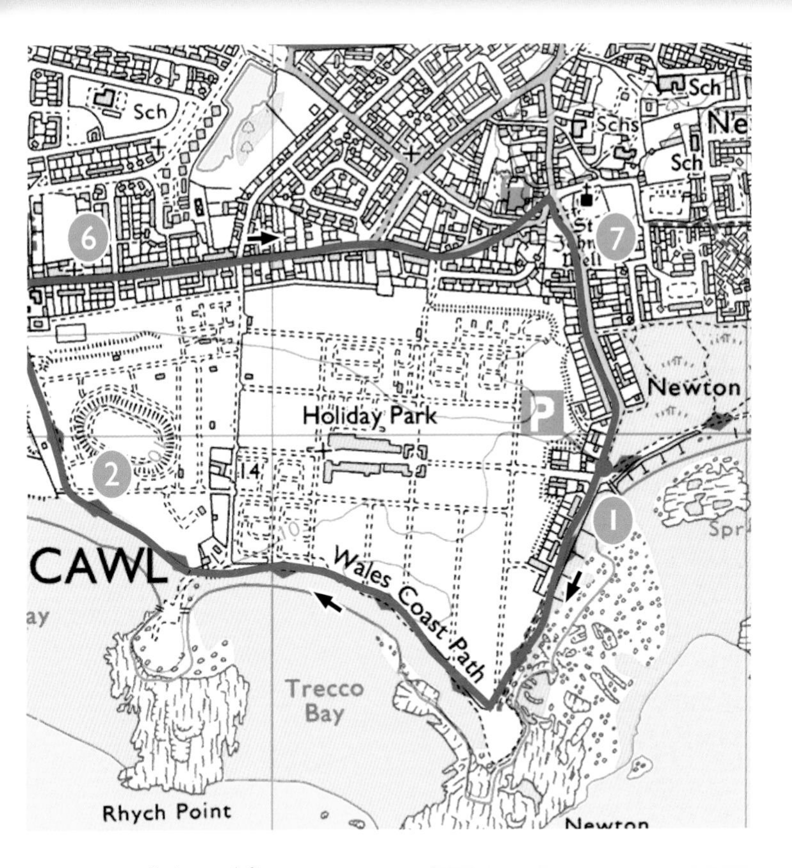

caravan site to your left.

3. At the end, pass a school on your right then turn right and immediately left. Go along the road to a roundabout and turn left by a play park and go along the edge of Sandy Bay on the esplanade.

4. Continue along the front, past pavement cafés and ice cream stalls. When you get to the impressive Art Deco Grand Pavilion, turn right. At the end of the road turn right then left and then right past the Co-op.

5. At the library turn right again to go down

the main shopping street. The museum is a little bit down the street on the right. At the bottom of the street you are back at the esplanade. Turn left to the roundabout and retrace your steps as far as the junction with the school.

6. Go past the school and follow a long residential street until you reach a pretty green with pubs and a church.

7. Go round the green and turn down Beach Road, passing the church and a play park to return to the car park. If you prefer to avoid the walk along the street, simply return by the beach from the junction at the school.

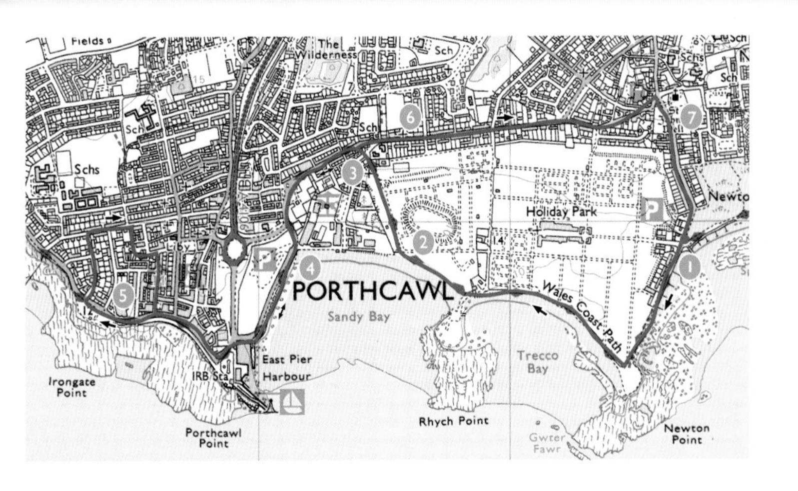
Fields
The Wilderness
Sch
Schs
Holiday Park
PORTHCAWL
Sandy Bay
Wales Coast Path
Trecco Bay
East Pier
Harbour
IRB Sta
Irongate Point
Porthcawl Point
Rhych Point
Gwter Fawr
Newton Point
Newton

PARC SLIP

A DELIGHTFUL NATURE WALK THROUGH A FORMER COAL MINING SITE. IT HAS BEEN TRANSFORMED WITH WETLANDS, HEDGEROWS AND HABITATS FOR A RANGE OF WILDLIFE. YOU COULD BE IN THE HEART OF THE COUNTRYSIDE, SURROUNDED BY HEDGES, BURBLING RIVERS AND BIRDSONG, YET YOU ARE NEVER FAR FROM THE VISITOR CENTRE.

It is hard to believe that this apparently natural haven is a reclaimed industrial site, once dominated by slag heaps and drift mines. A stark grey landscape, yet also the lifeblood of the people, who depended on the industry to live or die, as 112 men and boys did in the mining disaster of 1892. A memorial fountain in the park is dedicated to them. The pit closed in 1904, was mined again in the 1960s and finally restored to the beautiful nature reserve you see today in the 1990s.

Three species of newt are found around the ponds here. The Great Crested Newt is larger than the others, with dark coarse skin and orange underside. During the spring and summer breeding season, the males can be distinguished by a wavy crest running along their backs. In and around the ponds they feed on insects, larval nymphs, tadpoles and worms, all in plentiful supply. From late spring until autumn, you will see hosts of colourful dragonflies and damselflies everywhere. Dragonflies are larger and faster; damselflies fly lower, skimming the water.

Look out along the paths for piles of logs and sticks left to provide winter homes for the larvae of the glow worm. The glow worm is actually a beetle and only the female glows to attract the males. They are an endangered species so the nurturing of the glow worms spotted here is important.

Another important species to be found here are the orchids. The flower of the Bee Orchid, seen in early summer, resembles a bee to attract its pollinator, although in fact it self-pollinates. The Pyramidal Orchid, which appears in summer, has pyramid-shaped flowers and is pollinated by butterflies. The commonest orchid is the Marsh Orchid, which grows to over 2 feet (70cm) and is widespread in damp woodland areas.

This is just a tiny fraction of the wildlife that you can see here, without even mentioning the birds and mammals of the woods and wetlands. The variety of species is quite staggering, as you can see from the lists provided in hides and at the visitor centre.

THE BASICS

Distance: 2¾miles / 4.4km
Gradient: Negligible
Severity: Easy
Approx. time to walk: 2 hours
Stiles: Two but both have gates
Map: OS Explorer 151 (Cardiff and Bridgend)
Path description: Gravel and woodland paths, some duckboard
Start point: Parc Slip Visitor Centre car park (GR SS 880840)
Parking: Visitor Centre at Parc Slip, to the west of Tondu (CF32 0EH)
Dog friendly: Yes
Public toilets: At Visitor Centre
Nearest food: Café at Visitor Centre

1. From the visitor centre go through the gate onto a broad gravel path. At a fork where the cycle trail goes left, continue ahead. At the next junction, with a wooden sign indicating wildlife to be seen, turn left.

2. Go on here, winding round the path and over duckboards to a kissing gate. Go through and turn right through another gate towards a hide. As you approach the hide look over to the left to see the massive remains of opencast coal mining on the horizon. It is now overgrown and blends with the countryside.

3. From the hide you overlook a wide area of wetlands. Return to the gate and bear right on a grassy path between hedgerows. Look out for the glow worm hibernacula and glistening spiders' webs in the grass.

4. When you reach a stile, cross it and go right. At a sign for the Butterfly Ride to the left, go straight ahead across a stile. Continue on the path until you reach a broad gravel path and turn right.

5. Go along this path to a fork and take the right fork following the cycle trail. It winds round to a bridge on the right.

6. Cross the bridge and go along a delightful path between hedgerows and a stream with lots of little waterfalls. At the end of this path you reach the gravel path again and turn right. Take the next left to another hide by a lake.

7. Return to the road and turn left to continue along the gravel path. Turn left again at the next junction, passing some highland cattle to the left.

8. At the T-junction at a pond, you can go left to the hide or turn immediately right to return to the Visitor Centre along the canal. You emerge at the pond next to the Visitor Centre and the car park.

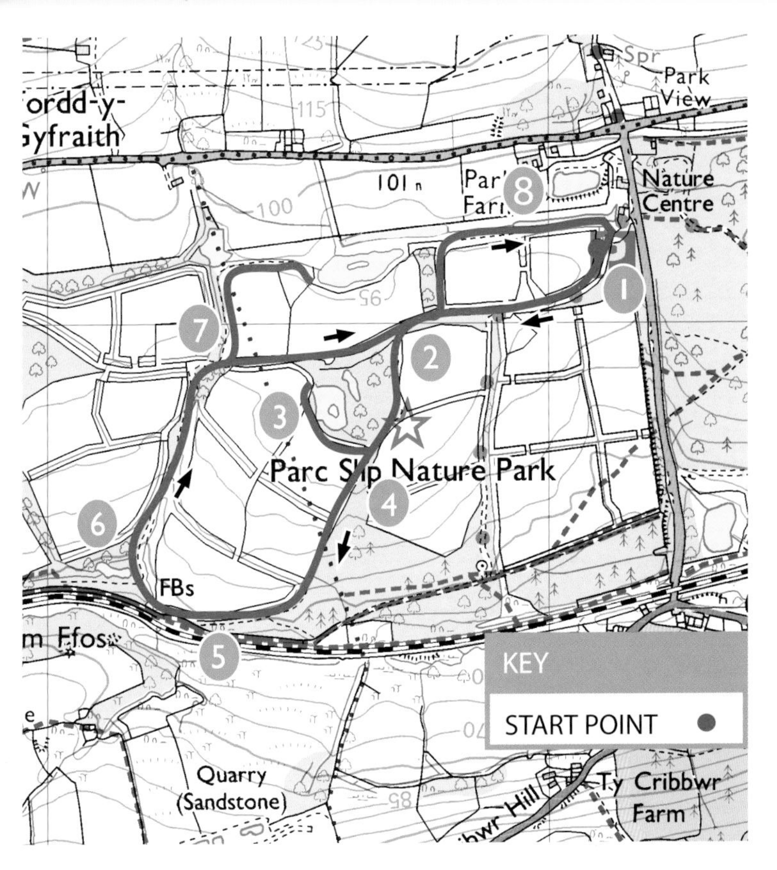
Park View
Spr
Nature Centre
Par Farm
101
115
100
95
Parc Slip Nature Park
FBs
Ffos
Quarry (Sandstone)
Ty Cribbwr Farm
KEY
START POINT

BRYNGARW

THIS WALK THROUGH A NATURE PARK GOES BY THE RIVER, THROUGH WOODLAND AND MEADOWS – AND DON'T MISS THE CHINESE GARDEN.

This must be one of the loveliest country parks in Wales. It still retains the feel of a country house park, with delightful corners to wander through, each divided from the rest by hedges and woodlands. The estate belonged to the Traherne family for generations, and the house, believed to be 15th century, was extensively modernised in the Victorian era. The formal garden was also designed and laid out by the Trahernes, including the Chinese Garden. However in the mid-20th century, the house was converted into flats and the garden fell into neglect until the 1980s, when it was gradually restored and opened as a country park in 1986.

The Chinese Garden, planted with trees from China and Japan, was created by Captain Traherne in the early years of the 20th century. It had become very overgrown, but to restore the park it was cleared and new Japanese Maple were planted to replace the old trees. The bridge over the ponds and the tea house were added to enhance the oriental feel. It is a particularly lovely and peaceful spot.

Another quiet and peaceful place is the lake, created in 1920. The lake is teeming with wildlife; there are roach, tench and rudd, which provide food for herons and kingfishers; there is a large colony of breeding mallards as well as winter visitors; spring sees frog, toad and newt spawn appear followed by a whole host of insects such as water boatmen, pond skaters, damselflies and dragonflies.

An unusual habitat, in these days of intensive industrial farming, is meadowland. Surrounded by ancient hedgerows, some of the grasses here are left to grow long enough to protect the wildlife; the tiny mammals scurry through; the wild flowers cling to the grasses; and clouds of butterflies flutter by.

If you have children with you, they will enjoy the play park in the middle, with its futuristic silver slide, which looks like a space rocket. But this play park is not just for children. For adults or teenagers there is an extensive outdoor gym, with clear instructions on how to use all the equipment, so if your walk through the park has been too leisurely and peaceful to burn the calories, you can enjoy a good workout here.

THE BASICS

Distance: 2½miles / 4km
Gradient: Gentle slopes
Severity: Easy
Approx. time to walk: 2 hours
Stiles: None
Map: OS Explorer 151 (Cardiff and Bridgend)
Path description: Woodland paths and grass
Start point: Bryngarw Country Park car park (GR SS 905852)
Parking: Bryngarw Country Park car park, just north of M4 junction 36 (CF32 8UU)
Dog friendly: Yes
Public toilets: At car park
Nearest food: Café at car park

BRYNGARW WALK

1. Follow the path through the car park away from the café to the wooden walkway. At the end of the walkway turn left through the forest on a narrow path. At a path junction turn right and then at a fork keep left. Keep on the path down some steps and along the path by the river. Continue by the river, looking out for a strange tree shape that looks like a snake and a wooden sculpture, 'Keeper of the River'. Turn right across a bridge and pass a cycle path, then cross a bridge and turn right.

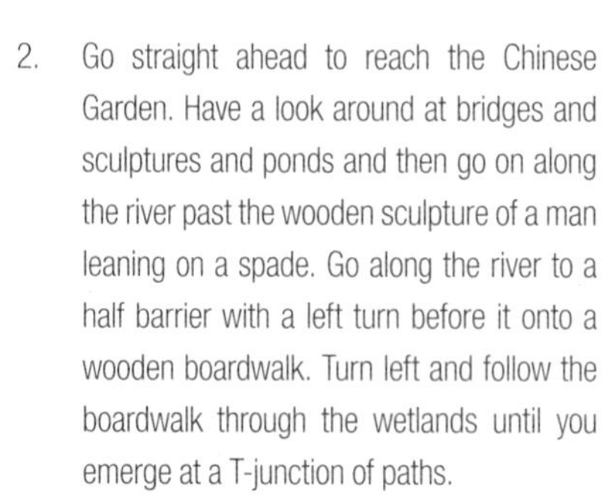

2. Go straight ahead to reach the Chinese Garden. Have a look around at bridges and sculptures and ponds and then go on along the river past the wooden sculpture of a man leaning on a spade. Go along the river to a half barrier with a left turn before it onto a wooden boardwalk. Turn left and follow the boardwalk through the wetlands until you emerge at a T-junction of paths.

3. Turn right and then right again at the next junction and then take a narrow path to the left with a green way-marker on it. Cross a bridge and go right and then right again to take the path into the woods. You will then come upon another wooden sculpture, 'The Keeper of the Woods'. Continue to follow the path as it winds up through the woods and down.

4. At a junction with a green way-marker turn right to head back towards the start. The path winds down through the woods to pass Bryngarw House and the lake.

5. At the lake turn right around the lake and go through towards the play park. Look for the path through a gap in the trees to the right of the lower slide and go through the gap and on into the meadow. As you go up you will see the wooden sculpture, 'The Keeper of the Meadow'. Continue on the path through another gap and around the meadow beyond.

6. Then follow the path back down to emerge behind the slide at the top of the pay park. Go through the play park and then have a look at the outdoor gym. You might like to try some of the activities. Then continue down back to the car park.

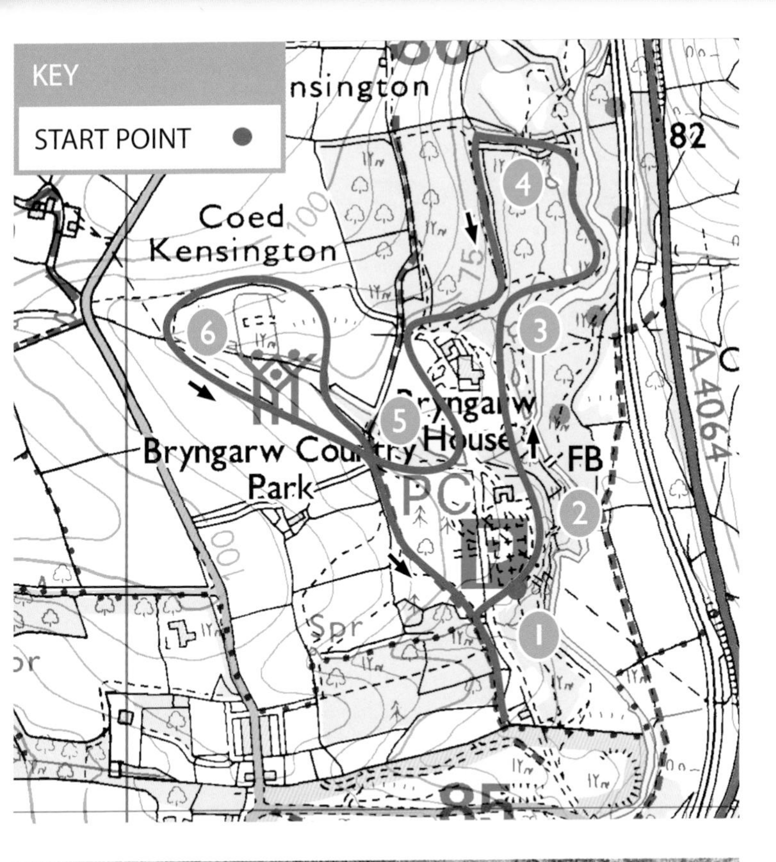
KEY
START POINT
Coed Kensington
Bryngarw House
Bryngarw Country Park
PC
FB
Spr
A 4064
82
75
100
1
2
3
4
5
6

TONDU

A walk around the best-preserved Victorian Ironworks in Wales then along the bed of an abandoned railway to the workers' houses.

The massive Ironworks in Tondu were established by Sir Robert Price in 1838 as the Glamorgan Coal and Iron Works. Price was MP for Herefordshire and despite being chairman of the Dyffryn, Llynfi and Porthcawl railway company, had no business acumen and even less experience of running a business. The ironworks was facing bankruptcy when it was taken over by John Brogden and Sons, a Lancashire firm of iron and coal masters. They successfully developed the mining, ironworks and railway business and continued to operate them until they went bankrupt in the 1880s. It was then acquired by one Colonel North. The new company, North's Navigation Collieries Ltd, put all its resources into coal production, continuing until the coal industry was nationalised in 1947. The Tondu Ironworks then became the West Wales Headquarters for the National Coal Board (NCB) until, in 1986, the NCB was privatised.

The old engine houses of the ironworks are now converted into offices for local businesses. On the site you can see the entrance to what was a drift mine, where coal was extracted after the works closed in 1895. The blast furnaces have long gone but you can see the furnace floor and the site of the cast house. Similarly the puddling furnaces, used to reduce the carbon content of the iron, are gone, as is the mill where the wrought iron was rolled into sheets and rails. The most interesting area is above and behind the engine houses. There you will find the calcining kilns, where the ore was roasted to prepare it for the blast furnace. In front of that is the lift, which took the ore, limestone and coke down to the furnaces. Coal was mined locally but before it could be used in the blast furnace it had to be converted to coke. At the rear of the calcining kilns you'll find the banks of beehive coke ovens for converting the coal to coke, some fully excavated, others barely visible.

The walk continues along the trackbed of the Dyffryn, Llynfi and Porthcawl Railway (DLPR). It was constructed in 1828, initially as a horse-drawn tramway that ran from Porthcawl for 17 miles along the Llynfi Valley. It is now a cycleway and links several of the walks in this book.

THE BASICS

Distance: 2½ miles / 3.6km
Gradient: Some gentle slopes
Severity: Easy
Approx. time to walk: 2 hours
Stiles: None
Map: OS Explorer 151 (Cardiff and Bridgend)
Path description: Road and paths
Start point: Tondu railway station (GR SS 895844)
Parking: Car park at Tondu railway station (CF32 9DR)
Dog friendly: Yes
Public toilets: Parc Tondu
Nearest food: Pubs on the route

1. Head onto the station platform, turn left then left again onto the footbridge. At the top turn left once more then descend the other side, keep ahead on the footpath then bear left along the road, then keep right to reach the T-junction beside the Llynfi Arms. Carefully cross the road then turn left to head along the pavement. Pass a filling station on the left, then turn right at the first junction.

2. Walk uphill a short distance then head towards a green sign, pass it to enter a car parking area and then continue across it, past a small pond on the left, to reach the gates of the former Iron Works. Go through a pedestrian gate and keep right on a path, which will lead you to reception. The Ironworks building is now offices but you can wander round the site. First go and sign in at reception and get hold of the leaflet with a site map.

3. Then come back down to the front of the works, cross an open area and head uphill on a footpath which will curve first of all to reach the side of the blast furnace. Then go back a little and continue on the path through the trees that will take you up another level to the back of the furnace. The path continues beyond that then turns right again to go around another area of the works, this time one that has not been fully excavated. From there you must return on the path back to the gate and exit the site. Now head back towards the end of the car park then turn right.

4. Go past a metal gate onto a lane then at a junction bear left onto a footpath and follow that to reach a metal gate, which you can pass. Then turn left onto the Celtic Cycle Trail.

5. This is the trackbed of an old tramway and you follow it past the turnoff for Tondu Park then continue until it becomes a wooden walkway. Just before the metal barriers at this walkway, bear right onto a narrow footpath that runs into the woods.

6. Keep on this until it reaches a T-junction, then turn right and go along a track to reach an area of gardens behind a row of terraced houses. Follow this to the end then turn left and round to visit the houses of Park Terrace, which are a typical example of the accommodation that the workers in the Iron Foundry would have had.

7. Then turn back and, keeping to the road, pass a children's play area and follow the road to reach a T-junction. Then turn right and go downhill. Keep on this until you see the

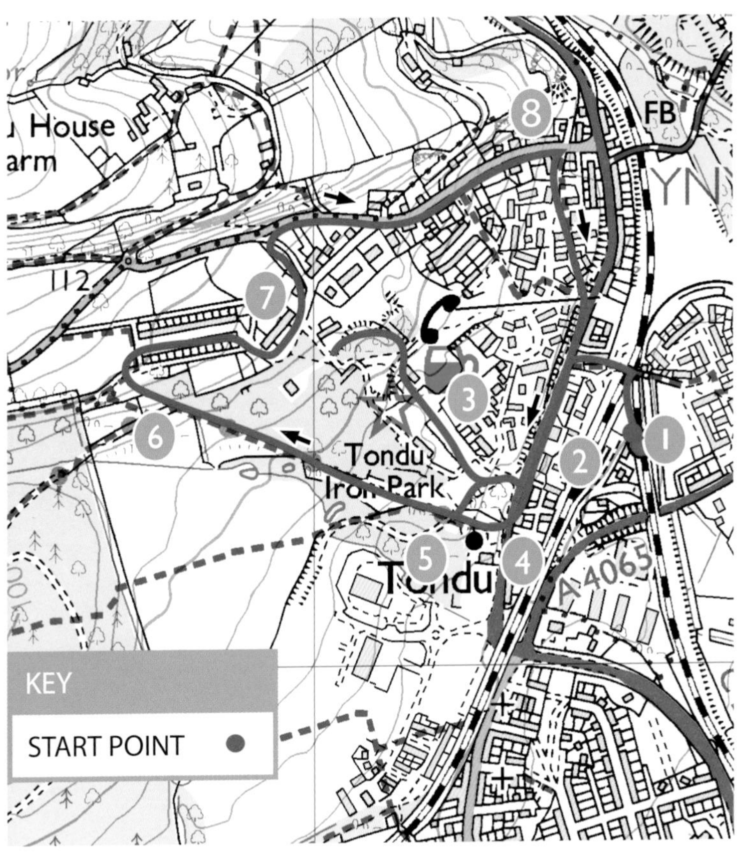

junction with the main road ahead then turn right into the street before.

8. The house on the corner to your right is called Lancaster House. Walk along the pavement on the left-hand side of the road. When the road turns, keep left along an alley between houses then, when the path turns left, keep ahead to go down some steps and onto the main road opposite a children's play area. Cross the road and continue for a few yards to the Llynfi Arms, then turn left to return to the start

BEDFORD PARK

A DELIGHTFUL PARK WALK ROUND THE REMAINS OF AN INDUSTRIAL REVOLUTION IRONWORKS AND A COUPLE OF OLD RAILWAYS.

Ironmaster John Bedford established the Cefn Cribwr ironworks in this park in the 1780s, the remains of which are now protected as a scheduled ancient monument, and it is one of the most complete of its kind in Britain.

The outward footpath through the park follows the line of the former Dyffryn, Llynfi and Porthcawl Railway encountered in the walk at Tondu. Originally constructed as a horse-drawn tramway, it is now the Celtic Cycle Trail, part of the National Cycle Network, and seven miles (11km) in length.

Walking through Bedford Park today it is difficult to envisage the noise, smells and dirt that would have been present when the ironworks was operational. Bedford was from Birmingham but he built his works here because of the natural resources available locally. He opened mines to gain access to the coal and ironstone that would be his raw materials. He also built brickworks and a large forge, so that his ironworks was almost completely self-sufficient.

Although Bedford had started in the iron trade and had a successful career that enabled him to purchase the site at Cefn Cribwr, he appears to have neglected the basics of business and instead concentrated on pushing forward the development of the iron-making process through experiments. As a result the ironworks never achieved the results that he had hoped for. After he died in 1791 it went downhill, but while iron making ceased the site continued to produce coal and manufacture bricks into the 20th century with the end coming just after the Great War.

Not far from the ironworks and included in this walk is the signal box at Cefn Junction.

This was part of the Llynfi and Ogmore Railway and only closed in 1973. It was scheduled for demolition but was saved by an organization called Y Cefn Gwyrdd, which had originally been formed to save the ironworks at Bedford Park. The restored signal box is home to an exhibition covering the history of the iron, coal and brick industries that were once prevalent here and, of course, the railways that were used to transport raw materials and finished product.

THE BASICS

Distance: 2½ miles / 4km

Gradient: Mainly level

Severity: Easy

Approx. time to walk: 2 hours

Stiles: None

Map: OS Explorer 151 (Cardiff and Bridgend)

Path description: Metalled and woodland paths, old railway track

Start point: Car park at Bedford Ironworks (GR SS 853834)

Parking: Car park at Bedford Ironworks, just north of B4281 at Cefn Cribwr (CF32 0BW)

Dog friendly: Yes

Public toilets: At Parc Slip Nature Park

Nearest food: The Farmers' Arms in Cefn Cribwr

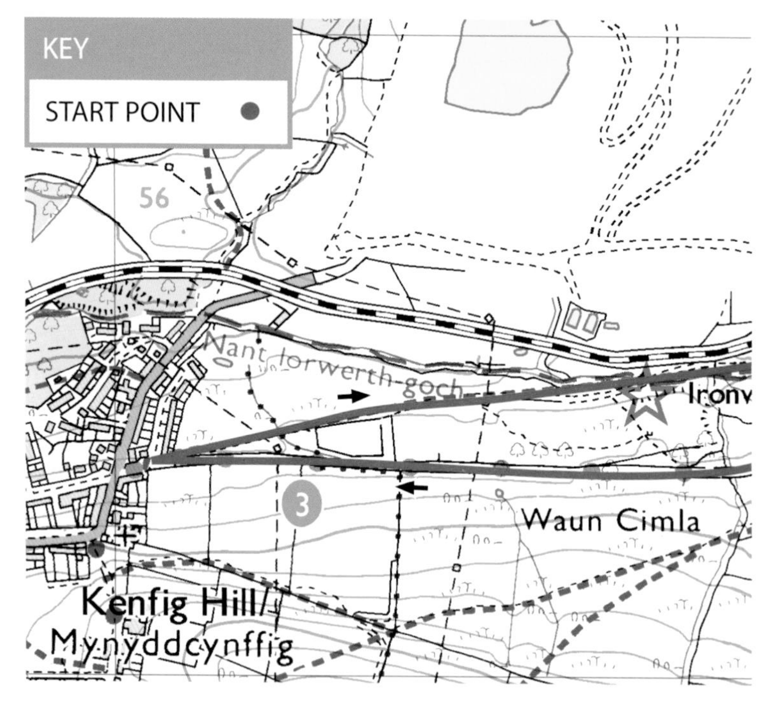

1. Exit the car park onto a well-paved footpath that starts from an interpretation board in the left-hand corner. Follow this to reach a wall, go through a gap stile and turn right onto a footpath. Keep on this to reach a way-marker post beside a junction and turn right onto a lesser footpath that leads to the railings round the top part of the Cefn Cribwr Ironworks Site. Have a walk round the excavated remains of a calcining kiln. You can then head downhill on the path to explore the rest of the ironworks, then return to the top.

2. When you have seen enough, continue on the footpath as it curves to the left to re-join the main path and continue along it. Keep on this path, which is part of

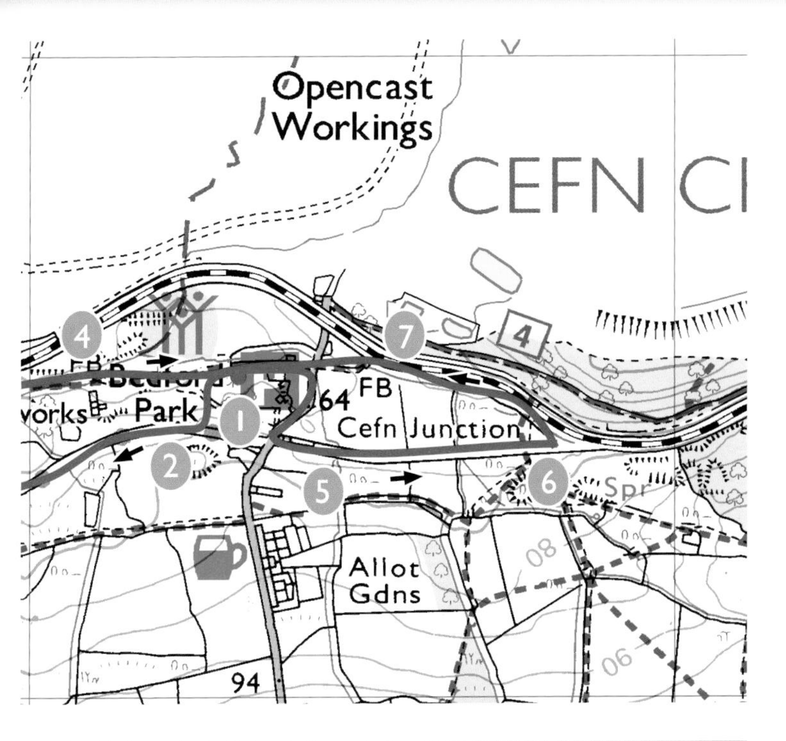

the National Cycle Network Route 4, to reach a barrier and gate across the path. Then turn right.

3. This footpath is a lot rougher and after turning right again continues back in the direction of the car park. There will be views across open countryside, sections of woodland, a stretch where it runs beside the railway and then a further section where there is a river on the right. Then cross the river on a footbridge and enter the grounds of the Ironworks. If you have not already explored this part then you can wander round the various buildings and read all about them on the interpretation boards. Then exit the railed compound and continue on the footpath.

4. This goes through a section of woodland. When you come to a junction you can turn right to return to the car park, but for the full walk keep ahead to pass a house on the left then exit via a gap stile onto a lane.

5. Turn right and walk along the lane, passing the entrance to the car park then turning left at the sign for Cefn Junction. Pass by a gate and walk along the bed of the old railway to reach the signal box, which is now a museum. It is only open on occasion as it is run by volunteers (see the website at www.ycefngwyrdd.co.uk). Nevertheless it is still worth a visit even when closed.

6. Return along the same route for a short distance then take a right turn at a crossroads of paths, go through a kissing gate and across a short field to go through another kissing gate, cross a footbridge, then the railway line and finally through another kissing gate then turn left onto a lane.

7. Follow this to the end near the remains of a cottage, turn left then go under a railway bridge and along a lane to return to the car park.

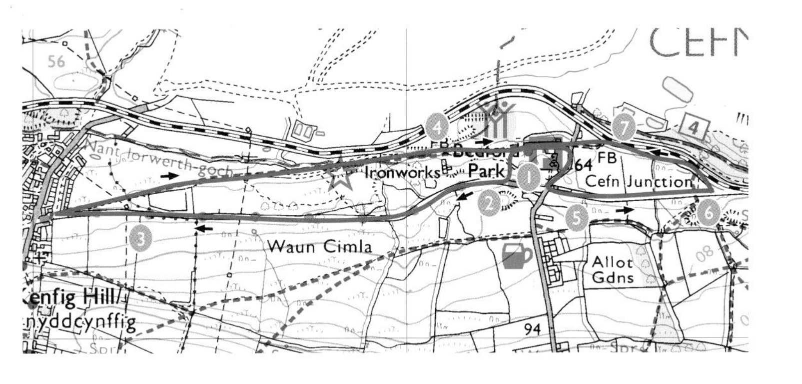
CEFN
Nant Iorwerth-goch
Ironworks
Park
FB
64
Cefn Junction
Waun Cimla
Allot
Gdns
Kenfig Hill/
Mynyddcynffig
56
94
4

CEFN JUNCTION SIGNAL BOX

COYTRAHEN

A WALK ON PAVEMENTS, OLD TRACKBEDS AND ACROSS OPEN COUNTRYSIDE TO EXPLORE THE VARIED HERITAGE THAT SURROUNDS THIS SMALL TOWN.

While this walk starts and ends in a village it is mainly in the countryside and through woodland. In the summer wild flowers bloom in profusion and carrying a pocket field guide will enhance the walk by encouraging children to see how many different kinds of flower can be identified. Other guides covering wild birds, insects and even a field guide to trees would be worth carrying to help to keep children of all ages occupied for the length of the walk.

The Nicholls Arms public house at the start of this walk is a Grade II listed building, originally opened as an inn in the mid-19th century on land belonging to the Merthyr Mawr Estate. The horse-drawn Dyffryn Llynfi Porthcawl Tramway ran along the contours of the hills behind the pub. It was the main artery connecting the Llynfi Valley Collieries and Ironworks with the docks at Porthcawl and was in use from 1825 to 1861. It changed to steam-powered locomotives after this and a new track was laid to the east of Coytrahen. Today it is part of the Maesteg to Bridgend line and the old tramway trackbed is part of this walk. Look out on that section for the trackbed of what was called Vaughan's Incline. It and the building below are all that now remain. It was constructed to connect two tramways and when it was no longer used the building became a shelter for travellers.

When you get to the bridge at point 2 look out for traces of Sir Richard Price's tramway and leet. Price had the watercourse built to supply his ironworks with water. It and the tramway once ran on parallel routes through Coytrahen. The woodland walk towards the end of the route is along the trackbed of Price's tramway.

When you leave this and turn left onto the main road again look out for the building on your left that was once a Methodist Chapel. Building of this commenced in 1900 and it was opened for worship on 1 March 1901. It cost £480 back then on land owned by Merthyr Mawr Estate. Later the freehold was bought from the estate. It closed in 1991 and is now a private dwelling.

THE BASICS

Distance: 2½ miles / 4km
Gradient: Gentle
Severity: Easy
Approx. time to walk: 2 hours
Stiles: Six
Maps: OS Explorer 151 (Cardiff and Bridgend) and 166 (Rhondda and Merthyr Tydfil)
Path description: Pavement, road, tracks, footpath and pasture
Start point: The Nicholls Arms in Coytrahen (GR SS 890857)
Parking: Nicholls Road, Coytrahen, near the Nicholls Arms (CF32 0EP)
Dog friendly: No; too many awkward stiles
Public toilets: No public toilets on route
Nearest food: Nicholls Arms

1. From the Nichols Arms turn left and walk along what looks like a crescent running beside the main road. At the end of this go up some steps and onto a public footpath. Follow this through the trees until it joins a track. Shortly after this bear right at a junction and head downhill on the Ridgeway Walk to reach a T-junction with the main road.

2. Turn right and very carefully cross the road. Then continue for a short distance along the grass verge and turn left onto a road signposted for Shwt Bettws and Llangeinor. This first crosses a railway bridge then comes to an older bridge over the river. At the end of this turn right at a footpath sign, go down some steps and cross a stile then continue along the right-hand edge of a field with the river on your right. Keep on the path as it enters woodland and then, just after it turns left, go right across a footbridge and through a kissing gate into a field. Veer left 45 degrees to cross the field to a stile that is a short distance to the left of a gate. Turn right onto a track and follow it to another gate. Go through this, then go left then almost immediately onto a footpath that goes uphill running parallel to the track. Keep on this to reach another stile, cross it then bear right and head diagonally downhill and into some woods. Then go along a track until it crosses some water then curves left. Turn right to go across a stile and into a field then keep ahead again to reach a bridge and a stile into woodland. From here follow the obvious path through the woods, cross another stile and continue by a fence across a boggy section of footpath to reach a cottage on your left. Shortly after that cross a stile onto the road and turn right.

3. Walk under the railway bridge then cross the river bridge and turn left onto the riverside path. Follow this until it ends then go up a set of steps and through a kissing gate.

4. Turn right onto a pavement and walk along the busy main road to re-enter the village. Just past the Coytrahen sign carefully cross the road to Cildaudy Road then turn right down a wooden walkway onto the Woodland Trail. Follow this to once again reach the main road, turn left and continue along it back to the start.

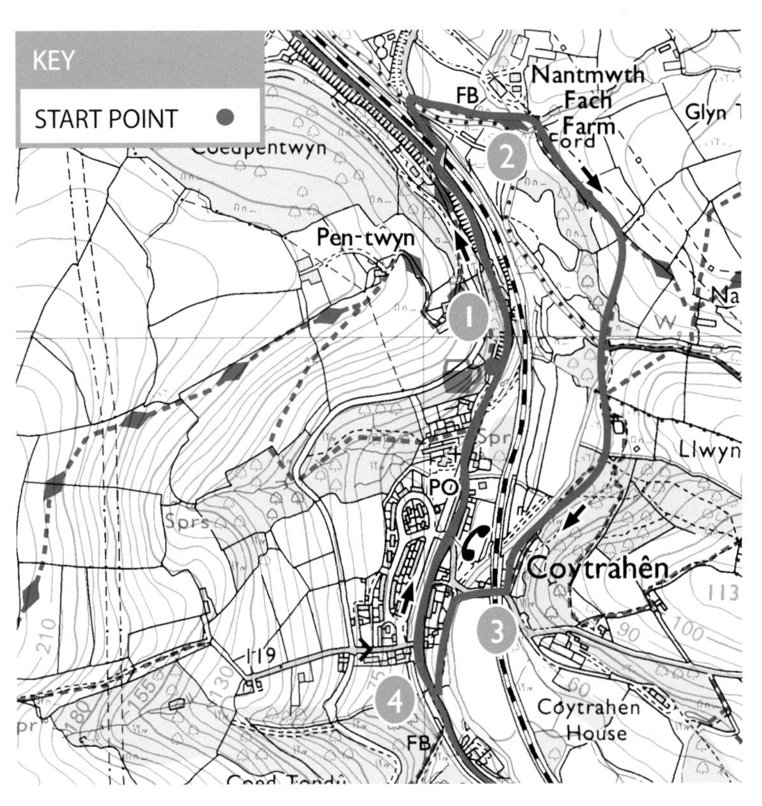
KEY
START POINT
Nantmwth
Fach
Farm
Ford
FB
Glyn
Coedpentwyn
Pen-twyn
Spr
PO
Sprs
Llwyn
Coytrahên
Coytrahen
House
FB
Coed Tondu
119
113
210
180
155
130
100
90
75
60
1
2
3
4

NICHOLLS
ARMS

A SPLENDID STROLL THROUGH BEAUTIFUL COUNTRYSIDE, WHICH STARTS AT ONE PUB AND ENDS AT ANOTHER.

One of the main claims to fame that the village of Coychurch has is its connection with the Reverend Thomas Richards, who compiled a Welsh to English dictionary in 1753. He rests for eternity in the corner of St Crallo's churchyard, which can be seen from the White Horse Pub. St Crallo's dates back to the 13th century. It is cruciform and has been described as 'an admirable model for a small colonial cathedral'. There has been considerable restoration work over the centuries but much of the original building is preserved. The other building of note in Coychurch is a modern crematorium. It is noted for its stained glass windows and because it was one of the last works of the notable English Modernist architect Maxwell Fry. He was famed for his 1937 creation, Kensal House in Ladbroke Grove, London, which he designed in collaboration with Elizabeth Denby a social reformer. He was also responsible for The Sun House in Hampstead, London; Margate and Ramsgate railway stations and the Pilkington Glass headquarters in Lancashire.

As you would expect from a walk in the country there are lots of natural things to look out for too. Take a short detour across the bridge at point 2 and explore Crematorium Wood. It's also called Coed Brynglas and contains mainly mixed broadleaves like oak and ash. Flowers to look out for are Herb Paris and Yellow Archangels. You might find it handy to carry a couple of pocket field guides, particularly if you have children with you. Birdlife is plentiful, particularly in the summer time, when there are lots of blue tits, long-tailed tits and great tits.

As you near the wood by Coed-y-mwstwr Ganol Farm at point 3 you are passing a place of legend. According to local lore this is where the body of King Arthur was brought after he was killed near Ogmore. His body was allegedly laid to rest in a cave in the woods and the death hushed up until his son was old enough to ascend the throne. Then it was announced and his body was disinterred and re-buried at Cor Emrys church, which was apparently not far from Coychurch.

THE BASICS

Distance: 4 miles / 6.4km
Gradient: Gentle slopes
Severity: Easy
Approx. time to walk: 2 hours
Stiles: None
Map: OS Explorer 151 (Cardiff and Bridgend)
Path description: Fields, roads and footpaths
Start point: The Prince of Wales pub, Coychurch (GR SS 938796)
Parking: At Prince of Wales pub or on street (CF35 5HD)
Landscape: Rolling fields
Dog friendly: Yes, but on lead through fields
Public toilets: At pubs in Coychurch
Nearest food: Pubs at start and finish

1. With the Prince of Wales on your right head along the road then turn right onto a footpath that runs between two walls and comes out in a cul-de-sac. Go along this then turn left into the street, cross over then take the first right turn. Cross the road again and then turn left at a footpath sign between a double-storey semi and a bungalow, just as the road starts to bend. Go through a gate at the end of the footpath, up some steps and, very carefully, cross the railway. Then go through another gate, down more steps and through a kissing gate into the field below. Follow the line of way-marker poles across this small field to go through a kissing gate to the right of a cattle grid, cross a lane and go through a kissing gate on the far side and into a field.

2. Turn right and follow the faint but obvious footpath to reach another gate, then continue over a second field. Pass a footbridge on your left and then go through another kissing gate, then keep right to reach a further kissing gate. Continue on the way-marked route through another two kissing gates. A large house, Lais House, can now be seen to your right. There's an electric pole in the next field, which is where you should head. Then cross the drive to Lais House, go through a kissing gate, cross a farm track and go through another kissing gate into a field.

3. Turn right at the gate and walk along the field with the hedge on your right. You should pass through four kissing gates on this section of footpath. After the first gate keep to the edge of the field with the fence on your left to reach gate two. Gates three and four are on either side of the access track between smallholdings 34 and 7. The waymarked path continues from here to another kissing gate beside a large tree. Go through and keep the edge of the field on your left to go through yet another gate and

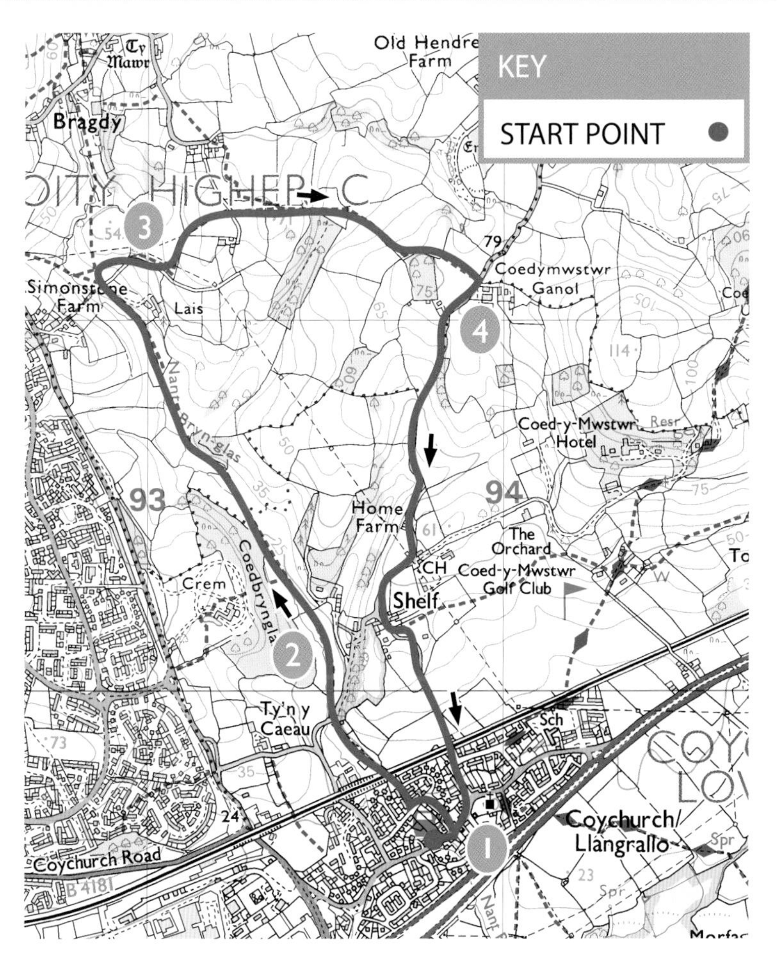

then proceed downhill towards the bottom left-hand corner of the field. There are three field gates there. Head towards the one in the middle. Go through it and then head uphill with the hedge on your right-hand side. Go through another field gate and, keeping the hedge to your right, then go straight ahead to a kissing gate opposite Coed-y-mwstwr Ganol Farm.

4. Turn right onto a lane. Keep on this passing Home Farm, Shelf Farm and then crossing the railway track again and keep going to reach the White Horse Pub.

Teeming wildlife and a medieval village at Cosmeston Lakes Country Park.

The lakes at Cosmeston are actually flooded quarries. They now attract masses of birds, filling the air with their whirling wings and spectacular dives for the food visitors bring. You are most likely to see mute swans, mallards, coots and the swift blue flash of the kingfisher. Visit in the winter to catch migrating birds such as teal, widgeon and shoveller ducks. There are many more and you'll find a list at the Visitor Centre of all the species of wildlife spotted in the park.

In the wetland you can see yellow flag iris and reed beds, providing habitats for dragonflies and damselflies. You can walk through the wetland on a boardwalk, providing a rare opportunity to observe this habitat close up. The extensive woodlands are mainly native species of oak, ash, elm and hawthorn and in the meadows around the edges appear first snowdrops and lesser celandine, followed by bluebells and many more as summer carpets the ground in wild flowers. The woodland is alive with birds and birdsong, particularly in the nesting season, from the sweet sound of tits and nuthatch to the tapping of the woodpecker and the harsh caw of the rooks. Look out too in the evening for the swift swoops of the bats as they catch gnats and other small insects. Rabbits and squirrels are easily seen as they run up trees or across paths, but there are many other animals, such as hedgehogs, voals and foxes, hidden in the woodlands. Again look at the Visitor Centre for the list of spotted species.

For a completely different experience, finish your visit to Cosmeston in the Medieval Village. If you are a Doctor Who fan or if you watched Merlin, you may recognise it, because it was used in filming for both of them. It was found when the park was being developed in 1978 and the archaeological remains have been rebuilt to provide as faithful a reproduction of life in the mid-14th century as you are likely to find anywhere. The Reeve's House is basic but compared to the ordinary villagers' it is very grand.

You can visit the baker's and the church and wander around the village green. There are guided tours and events to bring the past to life, but even without these it is a fascinating place.

THE BASICS

Distance: 3 miles / 4.8km
Gradient: None
Severity: Easy
Approx. time to walk: 1½ hours
Stiles: None
Map: OS Explorer 151 (Cardiff and Bridgend)
Path description: Well made-up paths
Start point: Cosmeston Lakes Country Park car park (GR ST 178691)
Parking: Cosmeston Lakes Country Park car park on B4267 south of Penarth (CF64 5UY)
Dog friendly: Yes
Public toilets: At Visitor Centre
Nearest food: At Visitor Centre

PENARTH WALK

1. Leave the car park and pass the Visitor Centre to enter the lakeside. Turn right onto the path and start walking round it anti-clockwise. Keep left at a junction and continue beside the lake. The path follows the water round the top of the Lake, passing a children's play area before reaching a T-junction with another path.

2. Turn right here. Keep along this long, straight footpath for some distance but keep a look out for a place where another footpath crosses it.

3. Turn left, go through a kissing gate and onto a path through scrubland. Then go through another kissing gate and into Cogan Wood. This area is teeming with birds and wildlife if you can stay still and silent long enough. Bring a bag of bird seed with you and scatter it on some logs or stones along the way. Keep a little way back and you'll soon be delighted by the display of blue tits and finches that come to dine. You are now on a broad, well-surfaced track. Keep on it, ignoring a minor turn-off to the right. At the end of Cogan Wood the track turns right then reaches a T-junction.

4. Turn left here then right at the next T-junction. This track will take you down between the two lakes, with lots of opportunities to have a look over the water.

5. When you reach the next crossroads turn left and walk along the back of the Medieval Village. When you reach the entrance to this turn right into it and spend at least half an hour exploring. Then continue on the path, which will take you back to the car park.

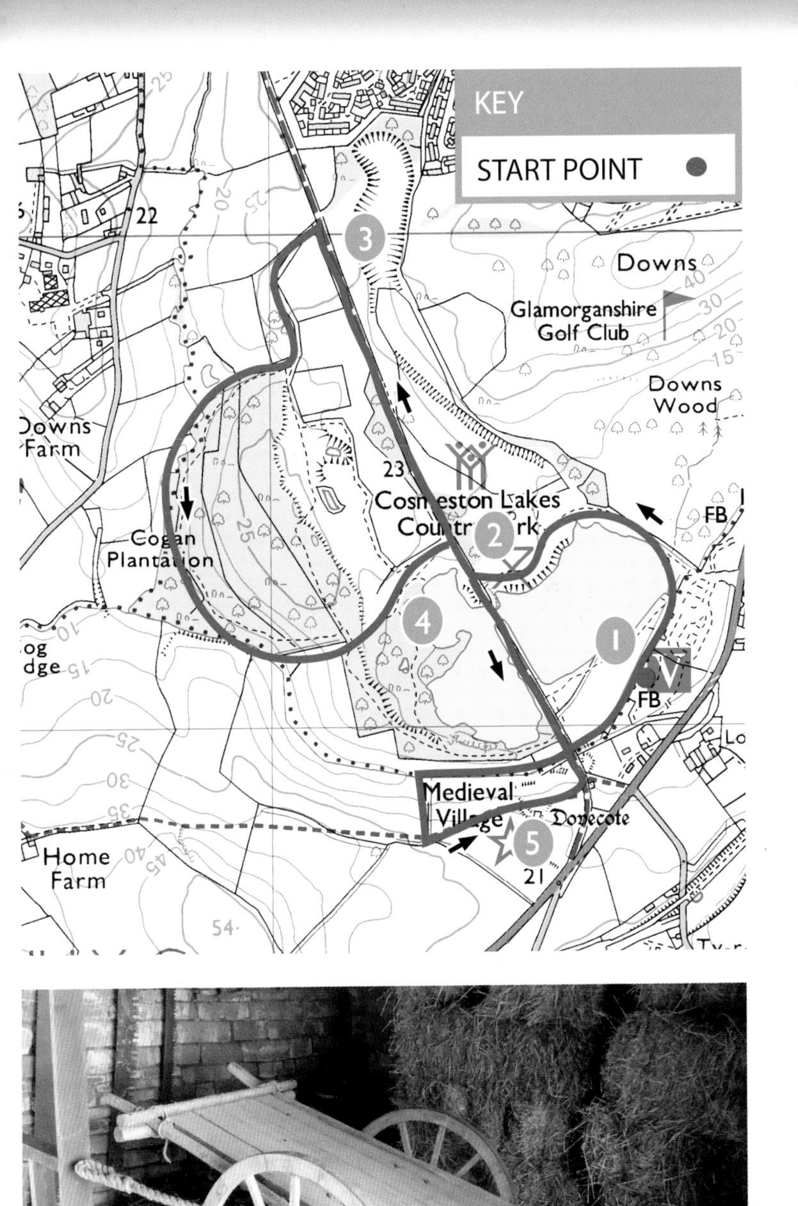
KEY
START POINT
Downs
Glamorganshire
Golf Club
Downs
Wood
Downs
Farm
Cogan
Plantation
Cosmeston Lakes
Country Park
FB
Medieval
Village
Dovecote
Home
Farm
22
23
21
54

ABOUT THE AUTHORS

Moira McCrossan and Hugh Taylor are a husband and wife writing team now specialising in travel for the over 50's and walking guides. They are also travel editors of the UK's premier over 50's web site laterlife.com.

Moira McCrossan spent most of her working life in education and was a Primary School Head Teacher. An active trade unionist she is a former President of the Educational Institute of Scotland, served on the general council of the Scottish TUC and the executive committee of the Women's National Commission for whom she co-authored the report, Growing up Female in the UK. She was also a frequent contributor to the Times Educational Supplement (Scotland).

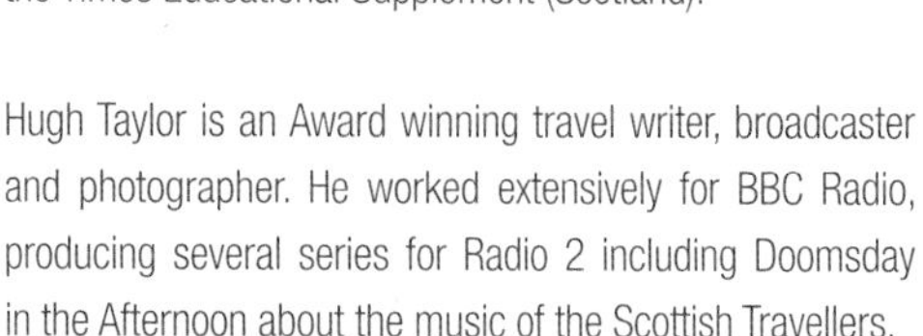

Hugh Taylor is an Award winning travel writer, broadcaster and photographer. He worked extensively for BBC Radio, producing several series for Radio 2 including Doomsday in the Afternoon about the music of the Scottish Travellers.

Together they have written or contributed to over forty travel and outdoor guides, some of which have been translated into several languages. They range from major country guides covering Scotland, Lebanon and Jordan to walking books throughout the UK. Their work has appeared worldwide in publications as diverse as The Times, Women's Realm, Choice, The Herald, Interval World and the Glencairn Gazette. They live in the picturesque southern Scottish village of Moniaive and in Capena, a hill town just north of Rome.

The Authors would like to thank Rob Ganley and the team at the Camping and Caravanning Club Press Office for all their help.